HIGHTIDE: THE PLAYS

HIGHTIDE: THE PLAYS

Steven Bloomer
YOU WERE AFTER POETRY

Megan Walsh
LYRE

Sam Holcroft
NED & SHARON

Sarah Cuddon
WEIGHTLESS

OBERON BOOKS
LONDON

First published in 2007 by Oberon Books Ltd
521 Caledonian Road, London N7 9RH
Tel: 020 7607 3637 / Fax: 020 7607 3629
e-mail: info@oberonbooks.com
www.oberonbooks.com

Cover design by Richard Dickinson

ISBN: 1 84002 740 1 / 978-1-84002-740-2

Printed in Great Britain by Antony Rowe Ltd, Chippenham

Contents

Contents

Introducing HighTide

OUR VISION FOR HIGHTIDE, founded in October 2006, is to provide a forum for young and emerging theatre artists in which they benefit both from the practical support of their established counterparts and from collaboration with their contemporaries. By building upon principles of trust and risk-taking, we aim to inspire, develop and realise powerful and provocative theatre. The idea behind the festival, where each of these plays received its première production, is to take plays from first draft to first performance, with a commitment to providing their authors and creative teams with sustained support throughout.

The four short plays printed in this book were chosen for full production at the three-day HighTide Festival in Suffolk from a pool of over fifty submissions. Four further plays were shortlisted and these received rehearsed readings. The unifying characteristic of all the shortlisted plays was the presence of a strong and unique voice with clear potential to be built on and developed. Following the selection, each shortlisted writer was paired with a director, and this creative partnership lay at the heart of the development process. In its early stages, this relationship can be fragile and sometimes overlooked. For this reason, each pairing was carefully mentored by an experienced dramaturg and supported by a host of practical and interactive masterclasses with leading writers and directors.

Since its inception, the company has grown both in size and diversity, incorporating the skills and passions of actors, designers, producers, technicians, musicians, photographers and film-makers. A genuine ethos of collaboration is the key to a sense of communal ownership, and one that we hope will go beyond the festival, inspiring partnerships and ventures in years to come. We believe that the future of British theatre, with the standards of excellence and influence that it has long boasted, lies not in the competitive isolation of solitary artists but in the ability to complement and build upon the talent and drive of others.

Sam Hodges
Artisic Director

The HighTide Creative Team are:

Artistic Director Sam Hodges
Creative Producer Lilli Geissendorfer
Creative Producer Moss Barclay

Literary Manager Mark Richards
Head of Writers Miriam Gillinson
Dramaturgs Paul Sirett & Richard Shannon

Head of Production Beth Hoare
Company Manager Hannah Ashwell
Casting Director Anna Cooper

Introducing the Festival

ART IS IMPORTANT because it slows a thing down long enough for it to be examined. The theatre, and art in general, should in England, as it is to a larger degree in other countries, be on what we used to call 'the national health'. The theatre is the one place remaining where anything can be said. Because nobody is likely to get rich, it is gleefully free for the most part from the commercial imperatives which can stifle writers in other mediums. I've been fortunate to be involved in the presentation of a number of new plays. A large part of the appeal is that you have the opportunity to deliver these plays for the first time.

In a world where we are increasingly required to accept unreliable accounts of our general progress we urgently need independent observers with fresh eyes and ears to honestly describe what in fact is going on. The HighTide Festival, in this its inaugural year, is crucial because it constitutes one of the few ways in which young playwrights in England are given the opportunity to see their work performed. In addition, the emphasis of the festival is on a development process which allows the new playwrights to learn from experienced writers and directors.

It is significant and refreshing that the HighTide Festival is taking place outside of the capital, or any of the other likely locations in England. It spreads the net further in terms of talent, and allows everyone involved – including the audiences – an excuse to visit one of the most beautiful parts of England. It allows new things to happen away from the pressure-cooker of London town.

Bill Nighy
Patron

Introducing the Writers

STEVEN BLOOMER trained as an actor at The Central School of Speech and Drama. He is currently part of Future Perfect 2006, a year-long attachment to Paines Plough Theatre Company. With Future Perfect he has written short plays for the Globe Theatre, the Trafalgar Studios and the Brighton Festival.

SARAH CUDDON is a producer/reporter for BBC Radio 4. As an undergraduate at Leeds University she co-founded Muchos Theatre. She has had poems published by *Rialto*, *Myslexia* and *New Writer* magazines and was recently *Tower Poetry*'s featured poet of the month.

SAM HOLCROFT was one of fifty writers nominated for the Royal Court Theatre and BBC Writersroom scheme 'The Fifty' in 2006. She has had short plays performed at the Southwark Playhouse, and is currently under commission to the Traverse Theatre, Edinburgh.

MEGAN WALSH has completed young writers' programmes at the Royal Court Theatre and the Soho Theatre, where she was shortlisted for the Westminster Prize in 2006. She has recently worked with the Battersea Arts Centre.

Steven Bloomer
YOU WERE AFTER POETRY

Characters

MAN

WOMAN

FIANCÉE

POET

SISTER

You Were After Poetry was first performed on 6 April 2007 as part of the HighTide Festival at The Cut in Halesworth, Suffolk, with the following company:

MAN, Chris Harper
WOMAN, Suzie Zara
FIANCÉE, Emily Gilchrist
POET, Geoff Breton
SISTER, Kate Donmall

Director Adam Barnard
Designers Josephine Callaghan
            Tanya Cunningham
Lighting Designer Lawrence Stromski
Sound Designer Steve Mayo

SCENE ONE

A bedroom in the city. Morning. A MAN and WOMAN are lying in bed together reading the Sunday papers. She is resting her head on his chest.

WOMAN: This is perfect.

MAN: Yeah.

WOMAN: Sunday mornings.

MAN: Yeah.

WOMAN: Favourite day of the week.

MAN: You comfortable?

WOMAN: Uh-huh.

MAN: Good.

(He waits for her to ask him. She doesn't.)

Anything interesting?

WOMAN: In the paper?

MAN: Anything?

WOMAN: No.

MAN: You sure you're comfortable?

WOMAN: Yes.

MAN: My chest isn't digging in to the back of your head?

WOMAN: What?

MAN: My chest, it isn't hurting your head is it?

WOMAN: No.

MAN: Good.

WOMAN: We seeing my sister later?

MAN: It's just that, it kind of feels like it might be hurting you.

WOMAN: It isn't.

MAN: Okay.

WOMAN: Are you okay?

MAN: What?

WOMAN: Comfy?

MAN: Me? Yeah. Yeah. 'Course.

WOMAN: Good.

MAN: No.

WOMAN: What?

MAN: It's just, the back of your head.

WOMAN: You're not comfy?

MAN: It's kind of digging in a little.

WOMAN: It's not comfortable?

MAN: It's a little…it kinda feels like you're giving me open heart surgery with the back of your head.

WOMAN: (*Getting up.*) I'm sorry.

MAN: It's fine.

WOMAN: You should have said, baby.

(*She starts to kiss his chest.*)

MAN: It's fine. Thank you.

WOMAN: I hurt my little baby.

MAN: It doesn't hurt.

WOMAN: I'm sorry.

MAN: It doesn't hurt.

(*She leans back against the headboard, his arm behind her.*)

WOMAN: Better?

MAN: Thanks.

(*She leans her head on his neck and they sit.*)

WOMAN: When we split up, we'll still be friends, won't we?

MAN: I'm sorry?

WOMAN: I mean, we're not going to be one of those couples who never speak to each other after they split up. 'Cause that would be a shame. Don't you think?

MAN: Are you splitting up with me?

WOMAN: Of course I'm not.

MAN: Then what are we talking about?

WOMAN: I'm just saying, hypothetically, when we split up –

MAN: Hypothetical is *if* not *when.* 'When' isn't a hypothetical.

WOMAN: Pedant.

MAN: Penis.

WOMAN: Pig.

MAN: Pillock.

WOMAN: Paedo.

MAN: Ouch.

(*The MAN starts to feel the weight of the WOMAN's head on his arm. He shifts position, wiggles his fingers.*)
You comfortable?

WOMAN: Fine.

MAN: Good.

(*He waits for her to ask him. She doesn't.*)

WOMAN: You think we'll still be friends?

MAN: *When* we split up?

WOMAN: *If.*

MAN: I hope so. Yeah, 'course we will.

WOMAN: Good. We could still hang out, you know, watch films together, all that stuff. We could maybe go on double dates together – how funny.

MAN: This conversation is surreal.

WOMAN: Why?

MAN: Well, I mean, isn't it? We're lying here, we've just had sex –

WOMAN: Good sex.

MAN: Great sex, and it's morning and London's looking beautiful and you're talking about going on double dates when we split up. Don't you think that's a strange topic of conversation?

WOMAN: No.

MAN: Right.

(*He looks worriedly at his fingertips; it's almost as if they're turning blue.*)

WOMAN: Realistically we both know we're not going to be together for ever.

MAN: Do we?

WOMAN: Don't we?

MAN: Well I don't know, we don't know yet.

WOMAN: Will you marry me?

MAN: What?

WOMAN: Will you marry me?

MAN: Will you just get off my fucking arm!

WOMAN: (*Turning to him.*) What?

MAN: (*Pulling his arm away.*) What are you doing?

WOMAN: Nothing!

MAN: It really hurts.

WOMAN: I'm sorry.

MAN: Are you proposing to me?

WOMAN: ⎤ What?
MAN: ⎦ What are you doing?

WOMAN: I'm not proposing to you.

MAN: You just asked me to marry you.

WOMAN: No I didn't.

MAN: My arm hurts.

WOMAN: Why didn't you say?

MAN: One minute you're talking about breaking up, next minute it's marriage.

WOMAN: I'm just talking.

MAN: But what does it mean?

WOMAN: Nothing, baby, just words, that's all.

MAN: Then why talk?

WOMAN: What?

MAN: Why talk if it means nothing?

WOMAN: I don't know. Why say you're comfortable if your arm hurts?

MAN: You're crazy.

WOMAN: You're…catty.

MAN: You're a cunt.

WOMAN: Ouch, you win.

MAN: I was happy.

WOMAN: What?

MAN: I was happy before, that's why I didn't say.

WOMAN: You can't be happy when someone's crushing your arm.

MAN: I was.

WOMAN: Don't lie to me.

MAN: Why did you ask me to marry you?

WOMAN: I didn't. I was asking if you would marry me.

MAN: How is that different?

WOMAN: I was asking if you see yourself, at some point in the future, marrying me.

MAN: Why would you ask that?

WOMAN: Because at some point in the future I see us breaking up.

MAN: You do?

WOMAN: Well I don't actually see us breaking up, I just see us with other people, that's all.

MAN: So you don't love me.

WOMAN: No!

MAN: No?

WOMAN: Does everything have to be so black and white?

MAN: You don't want to marry me, ever, you imagine us in the future being with other people, what are we even doing together? Are we just fooling around?

WOMAN: I do love you.

MAN: I could be with other women if I wanted to fool around.

WOMAN: Are you saying I'm bad in bed?

MAN: I'm saying I could be with other women.

WOMAN: I'm good in bed.

MAN: You're great in bed.

WOMAN: Then what's your problem?

MAN: I thought this was more than that.

WOMAN: It is, baby.

MAN: How can it be?

WOMAN: Because it is.

MAN: That's a shit answer.

WOMAN: Tough.

MAN: Marry me.

WOMAN: What?

MAN: Marry me. Please. Will you marry me?

WOMAN: Now?

MAN: Yes.

WOMAN: No.

MAN: Marry me or dump me.

WOMAN: What are you doing?

MAN: Marry me or dump me.

WOMAN: You don't have to do this.

MAN: Marry me or dump me.

WOMAN: I can't marry you.

MAN: Fine.

INTERLUDE ONE

These voicemail messages should be spoken on stage.

MAN: (*On voicemail.*) Hi. It's me. Erm, I know you said not to call you, or e-mail or…and I know you're probably not listening to this but I think it's important, and I think you'd want me to call you because, well, what I'm trying really to say is, I found some of your pants. And I was thinking of throwing them out but they're a nice pair, one of your nicer pairs I think, and I thought you might be missing them. So I've got them. I've not washed them. I didn't know if you wanted me to wash them, I can. So call round and get them, whenever, I think you've still got a key you can call round or I can post them to you or your sister or, you know, maybe we can meet up sometime and I can give them to you in person, whatever, it's just, they're one of your nice pairs so… Why do we say a pair of pants? Do you know? Because there's only one, it's not like socks… They're here, anyway, and that's all I wanted to say. I've got your pants. And I still love you.

SCENE TWO

The private meeting room of a bank. Afternoon. The MAN sits opposite an elegantly dressed woman. He is looking extremely tired.

FIANCÉE: I think it's disgraceful. I think it's absolutely and utterly disgraceful of you, of your bank – I've been a customer of yours for fifteen years.

MAN: Yes.

FIANCÉE: I have an account with this bank, I have credit cards with this bank, my fiancé's got an account with this bank – I've had an account with this bank for fifteen years.

MAN: Yes.

FIANCÉE: I think this is perfectly disgraceful.

MAN: You said.

FIANCÉE: I think this is perfectly disgraceful and what's more as soon as I'm married we will be taking our business elsewhere.

MAN: I'm very sorry to hear that.

FIANCÉE: This is the most important day – I know that's a cliché – of my life.

MAN: Yes.

FIANCÉE: Are you married?

MAN: I'm not, no.

FIANCÉE: Can I speak to someone who is married, please?

MAN: There's only me here.

FIANCÉE: I think I need to speak to someone who is already married.

MAN: What does your fiancé say about this?

FIANCÉE: What does it have to do with him?

MAN: Harry's a very wealthy man. Can't he pay for the wedding?

FIANCÉE: Do you know Harry?

MAN: Not personally, no.

FIANCÉE: Harry's a traditionalist. It's one of the reasons I love him. The bride's family pays for the wedding.

MAN: I see.

FIANCÉE: So, please, I'm asking you again, is there anything you can do? It's not a lot of money.

MAN: It is quite a lot of money.

FIANCÉE: We've already made reservations. We've booked a bishop. There's a string quartet flying in from Vienna. Harry's just mad about string quartets.

MAN: It sounds lovely.

FIANCÉE: Yes. Yes, it does.

MAN: I'm sorry there's nothing we can do to help.

FIANCÉE: This wedding is the most important thing in my life, the only thing, right now.

MAN: I appreciate that.

(*She undoes a button on her blouse.*)

FIANCÉE: Are you in love?

MAN: Yes.

FIANCÉE: Then you must understand how deeply I need this money.

MAN: Not really, no.

FIANCÉE: Can't you imagine yourselves getting married?

MAN: Not at the moment.

FIANCÉE: Why not?

MAN: She's a bitch.

FIANCÉE: Well that doesn't sound much like love to me.

MAN: It is.

(*She leans in and touches his knee.*)

FIANCÉE: How can I persuade you to lend me the money?

MAN: There's not really much you can do.

FIANCÉE: There's a lot I can do.

MAN: It's an automated system.

FIANCÉE: Shall I lock the door?

MAN: What?

FIANCÉE: The door – shall I lock it?

MAN: You can't.

FIANCÉE: I won't tell.

MAN: No, I mean you can't. There isn't a lock on that door.

FIANCÉE: We'll just have to hope nobody walks in then, won't we?

MAN: What are you suggesting?

FIANCÉE: Don't you find me attractive? I find you attractive.

MAN: Do you?

FIANCÉE: I like your hair.

MAN: You're about to get married.

FIANCÉE: Look at me. Look me in the eyes. This wedding is the only thing I've got.

MAN: I haven't slept for three days.

FIANCÉE: It has to be beautiful.

MAN: I don't know if I know what you're saying to me.

(*She kisses him.*

He kisses back then pushes her away.)

What are you doing?

FIANCÉE: Please, just lend me the bloody money.

MAN: I can't!

FIANCÉE: Harry will pay you back.

MAN: After you're married.

FIANCÉE: Harry's money will be my money.

MAN: I can't accept that.

FIANCÉE: Why not?

MAN: Because I don't think your marriage is going to last.

FIANCÉE: What?

MAN: At least not long enough to pay off the interest.
(*She slaps him.*)
I'm sorry. Would you like a drink?
FIANCÉE: No!
MAN: Perhaps you should.
FIANCÉE: Why?
MAN: It might help.
FIANCÉE: With what?
MAN: Your fiancé's having an affair.

I'm sorry to have to break it to you like that.
FIANCÉE: What do you mean Harry's having an affair?
MAN: I did offer you a drink.

FIANCÉE: With who?
MAN: I can't tell you.
FIANCÉE: Why not?
MAN: It's confidential.
FIANCÉE: How do you know?
MAN: He has payments coming out of his account every week to another woman, he rents a flat for this woman in town and he is often buying expensive gifts. When our system notices things like this it flags them up for our attention.
FIANCÉE: Are you sure?
MAN: We're a hundred per cent. It's computerised.
FIANCÉE: The bastard.
MAN: I shouldn't be telling you this, but, you see, I couldn't really lend you the money.
FIANCÉE: He makes figurines.
MAN: What?
FIANCÉE: The little wedding figurines for the top of the cake, Harry makes them, he's the biggest supplier of wedding figurines in the EU.
MAN: That's…ironic.
FIANCÉE: No, it's not, it's shit.
(*She starts to gather her things.*)
Fine, right, fine.
MAN: I'm really sorry.
FIANCÉE: You're certain about this?

MAN: I'm afraid so.

FIANCÉE: You can't lend me any money?

MAN: What?

FIANCÉE: You can't give me any money, is that what you're saying?

MAN: Do you still want to marry him?

FIANCÉE: Of course I want to marry him.

MAN: How can you still want to marry him?

FIANCÉE: You don't understand. Harry's an old bore. I've kissed most men in his office.

MAN: Have you?

FIANCÉE: And in his car, their car, their flat.

MAN: Then why do you want to get married?

FIANCÉE: Because I've made all these plans.

MAN: So?

FIANCÉE: And – and it's better than being alone. Isn't it? Isn't it better than being alone?

MAN: Maybe.

FIANCÉE: Maybe.

MAN: Maybe we can get you the money.

FIANCÉE: Thank you.

INTERLUDE TWO

WOMAN: (*On voicemail.*) Listen, I don't want the pants, I'm single now and I'm buying new pants. Pants you've never seen. And they're all nice pants now. There's no plain pants anymore, they're all nice pants. So I don't want them back but…but here's the thing. I don't want you to keep them. I know that sounds silly and I know, I know you're not some pant fetishist but I don't like you having my pants anymore so that's why I'm calling. I'd like you to throw them out or…or burn them. Preferably burn them, if it's not too much trouble. So I hope you haven't washed them yet because that would be a waste of time. Thanks.

Oh by the way, we say a pair of pants because they consist of two independent but connected parts, the front and the back, like a pair of scissors. It goes back to the thirteenth century when people talked about 'a pair of hosen'. Hosen are trousers. Don't tell me you love me ever again.

SCENE THREE

The original WOMAN follows a different man into a bedroom. The man wears a cravat and velvet jacket.

WOMAN: This is where you work?

POET: Work, play, live, die – exist, I like to say.

WOMAN: Yes, exist, yes.

POET: Take your coat off, you look…

WOMAN: Sexy?

POET: Radiant.

WOMAN: Radiantly sexy?

POET: There are some women who wear their beauty like a suit of armour. It weighs them down. They wear it with the self-consciousness of a ball gown or an ostentatiously decorated hat. But you wear yours like a veil, you seem unaware of it, only do you know that it cools you and keeps the smoke out of your eyes.

WOMAN: I'm not sure whether that's the nicest thing anyone's ever said to me or the biggest load of shit I've ever heard.

POET: Don't you believe me?

WOMAN: That's not what I'm saying.

POET: Why don't you believe me?

WOMAN: Its borderline is what I'm saying.

POET: Borderline?

WOMAN: On that kind of sexy/sleazy borderline.

POET: Oh.

WOMAN: Dirty/dingy borderline.

POET: So it could be nudged one way…

(*He touches her neck.*)

WOMAN: Maybe.

POET: …or the other way…

(*He runs his hand down her back.*)

WOMAN: Oh, yes. Yes it could definitely be nudged that way.

POET: Until it's no longer borderline, until, you could say, until it finally reaches home territory.

WOMAN: We welcome it to home territory!

(*She throws herself on him.*)

POET: Wait.

WOMAN: What?

POET: Shhhh.

(*He steps back and looks at her.*)

WOMAN: (*Half-whispered.*) Why?

POET: Because I think…I think you're the answer.

WOMAN: Good.

(*Still whispered.*) What's the question?

POET: Sometimes I sit in this room and I get this falling feeling that all my beliefs, all my philosophies so ceaselessly and constantly put forward and re-examined, are a moment of clarity in an argument far greater than anything paper can ever hold. It is as if I were hurtling through life on a high-speed train looking out of the window, and for a moment, passing by, I see a man in a nearby field who may be God or my father or the fishmonger holding up a sign on which is written the answer to the world and who is gone before I have properly seen him and who, I begin to doubt, I may not have seen at all.

WOMAN: (*The energy gone out of her.*) Right.

POET: When I look at you I realise…I realise I'm looking at the answer. You. You're my answer to the world.

WOMAN: Are you for joking?

POET: What?

WOMAN: Are you saying all this shit for real?

POET: Yes.

WOMAN: Oh.

POET: Why?

WOMAN: Right.

POET: This is what you wanted, right?

WOMAN: Well I don't know; I'm not sure now.

POET: This is what you said you wanted. What you were looking for.

WOMAN: I hadn't really envisioned it clearly. Not in any detail.

POET: I mean, I thought this was what you wanted. We can do it different if you want, I mean, I can do it differently.

WOMAN: No – I don't know.

POET: I just thought, I thought this was what you wanted. You said you wanted someone to be romantic and, you said poetic, and I just followed my instinct. Was it not that?

WOMAN: No, no it's good.

POET: I can do it differently.

WOMAN: I don't know.

POET: How should I be – more edgy?

WOMAN: How old are you?

POET: You don't ask that.

WOMAN: What's your name?

POET: You don't ask that.

WOMAN: What do you do?

POET: I'm a writer.

WOMAN: What do you really do?

POET: Poems, plays, everything, nothing.

WOMAN: Forget the role-play, what do you really do?

POET: Forget it?

WOMAN: Can't we just fuck? I mean, isn't that why you're here?

POET: I don't…I don't know.

WOMAN: That's why I'm here.

POET: I don't… It feels really weird without the roles.

WOMAN: Thought you said you'd done this a lot?

POET: I have.

WOMAN: You don't look like you know what you're doing.

POET: You might have to give me a moment. Can we just talk for a moment?

(*The WOMAN sits down.*)

Thank you.

I have done this a lot. I've done this loads.

WOMAN: I believe you.

POET: Is this your first time?

WOMAN: Yes.

POET: Why did you…?

WOMAN: Do you have to ask?
POET: No.
WOMAN: Good.

Break-up.
POET: I see.
WOMAN: Not uncommon?
POET: Not really.
WOMAN: I thought so.

POET: He's an accountant, your break-up?
WOMAN: He works for a bank.
POET: Yes.
WOMAN: How did you – you don't know him do you?
POET: Eight 'til six, wears a suit? You wanted to shag a romantic poet; I didn't think it was likely you'd just split up with Keats.
WOMAN: Am I that predictable?
POET: It's not a bad thing.
WOMAN: Isn't it?
POET: Clichés are clichés for a reason.
WOMAN: Thanks.

What do you do, really?
POET: I'm an actor.
(*She laughs.*)
WOMAN: Really?
POET: Trying to be.
(*She's still laughing.*)
I'm trained!
WOMAN: Not that… It's just – you're an actor on a role-play sex-site?! Bit of a busman's holiday isn't it?
POET: I like it.
WOMAN: That's hilarious.
POET: Do you miss him?
WOMAN: (*Suddenly stone.*) What?
POET: The banker?
WOMAN: Do you find me attractive?
POET: Yes.

WOMAN: What did you first think when you saw me? Did you notice my breasts?

POET: I'm not sure.

WOMAN: You must know. Downstairs, in the lobby – what was the first thing you noticed?

POET: Your eyes.

WOMAN: My eyes?!

POET: Yes.

WOMAN: And you thought I was cliché?

POET: Do you want to – ?

WOMAN: I'm not sure.

POET: We can do it without the roles.

WOMAN: I don't know which is worse. Or better. Whatever.

POET: What's your name?

WOMAN: Why?

POET: Just curious.

WOMAN: Thought you didn't ask that?

POET: Seems strange calling you Randy Rapunzel now that we're just sitting here.

WOMAN: Catherine. Cathy.

POET: I'm –

WOMAN: Don't tell me yours. Sorry.

POET: Okay.

   (*The WOMAN leans in and kisses him.*)

   Do you love him?

   (*She carries on kissing him.*)

WOMAN: I love you.

POET: That's not true.

WOMAN: Who cares if it's true?

POET: Do you still love him?

   (*She stops.*)

WOMAN: How many times have you done this?

POET: About thirty.

WOMAN: Why?

POET: I like it. I get lonely.

WOMAN: I get lonely.
POET: It's good for that.
WOMAN: You're still lonely though.
POET: Yes.
WOMAN: Why's that?
POET: I guess I'm the type.
WOMAN: I'm not.
POET: Good.
WOMAN: I'm not the lonely type.
POET: Good. That's good.

Fireman, plumber, delivery boy, postman, milkman, rat
catcher, knight in shining armour –
WOMAN: Rat catcher?
POET: This is my first poet.
WOMAN: Well I'm sorry. Sorry it wasn't what you expected.
POET: It's not anyone's fault.
WOMAN: Well I'm sorry anyway. You took the afternoon off
work.
POET: I'm only temping.
WOMAN: Still.
(*He gets up and starts to collect his jacket.*)
POET: I should go.
WOMAN: Don't go.
POET: This was weird.
WOMAN: Do you want me to pay for the room?
POET: No. They know me, I get a discount.
WOMAN: Right.
POET: Right. Good luck with the banker. Or not. Whatever.
WOMAN: Whatever.
POET: Thank you.
WOMAN: For what?
POET: Well…yes.
(*He exits.*
She stays in the room.)

INTERLUDE THREE

MAN: (*On voicemail throughout the interlude.*) Hi, I got your message, I hadn't washed them so no worries, I just wanted to let you know I've done it.

WOMAN: (*On voicemail throughout the interlude.*) Hi, I got your message. Thanks for burning my pants.

MAN: I'm not sure about your answer, we say 'a shirt' but that's got two sides and has two sleeves like trousers and pants.

WOMAN: On your question, shirts are mainly thought of as covering the torso and may or may not have sleeves. Pedant.

MAN: I know you don't want me to see you but I was wondering if I could see you.

WOMAN: You can't see me.

MAN: I'm not going to ask you to marry me.

WOMAN: I'm moving on, I'm happy. We were never happy, not really.

MAN: I just keep thinking about how happy we were.

WOMAN: I don't understand how you can say we were happy.

MAN: But then I think maybe happiness is different for different people. I was happy just lying in bed with you.

WOMAN: You were never happy lying in bed with me.

MAN: You always wanted something more.

WOMAN: How can you say this to me? You were always the one pushing for more.

MAN: You were always after – I don't know what you were after.

WOMAN: I wasn't after anything.

MAN: You were after poetry.

WOMAN: It was you who wanted these things, wedding bells and Sunday papers and walking in the park in the autumn wind.

MAN: I think we could try again.

WOMAN: I hate the fucking park. It's just cold and death and dead leaves everywhere. I only went because of you.

MAN: I think we could try again.

31

WOMAN: Somebody asked me my name today and for a moment I forgot. I don't know who I am anymore. I don't know who I've been playing for the last year but it wasn't me. That can't be love, can it?

MAN: I think we could try again.

WOMAN: Love isn't lying in bed and pretending your arm doesn't hurt.

MAN: I think we could try again.

WOMAN: Love is what comes after parks and poetry. Love is 'I sometimes fantasise about other people', it's – yes – it's 'get off my arm, my fucking arm hurts'. This is love. This is what I wanted. You can shove your dead leaves up your cunt.

SCENE FOUR

A late-night coffee shop in the city. The original MAN and the original woman's SISTER are sitting opposite each other. He's toying with the sides of his water glass and she's eating her cappuccino.

SISTER: Jesus, Mark.

MAN: Please.

SISTER: She doesn't want to see you.

MAN: I'm a mess.

SISTER: She really doesn't want to see you.

MAN: I'm in such a mess.

SISTER: That's one of the reasons she doesn't want to see you.

MAN: Fine.

SISTER: Can we talk about something else now?

MAN: Fine.

SISTER: Good.

MAN: How's she doing?

SISTER: For Christ's sake!

MAN: I'm worried about her.

SISTER: She's fine.

MAN: I haven't seen her for three days.

SISTER: She's really fine. She's well.

MAN: I brought her something.

(*He puts a small urn on the table.*)

SISTER: What is it?

MAN: It's her pants.

SISTER: Are you alright?

MAN: Is she seeing anyone?

SISTER: Can we talk about something else please?

MAN: Alright.

SISTER: Good.

MAN: Okay.

How are you?

SISTER: I'm well.

MAN: Good.

How's it working out having her stay?

SISTER: Mark.

MAN: What? That's about you.

SISTER: Hardly.

MAN: It is.

SISTER: Good. It's working out good. There's this man at work that I like.

MAN: Did you talk to him?

SISTER: He thinks I'm odd looking.

MAN: He doesn't.

SISTER: I think he likes someone else more.

MAN: You should talk to him.

SISTER: I think he thinks my hair looks stupid. My sister was always the one people liked.

MAN: Just because me and your sister – we're still friends aren't we?

SISTER: Well I'm sitting here.

MAN: Good.

SISTER: Just no more questions.

MAN: How's she looking?

SISTER: Fucking hell!

MAN: That was a joke! Jesus.

Who's this man?

SISTER: He's more of a boy.

MAN: A boy?

SISTER: One of our temps.

MAN: How young is this boy?

SISTER: I'm being serious.

MAN: You really like him?

SISTER: I don't know. I'm not very good at this.

MAN: Who is?

SISTER: I don't know. Other people.

MAN: What's he like?

SISTER: He's nice, he's – he took the afternoon off work today and I missed him.

MAN: Ask him out.

SISTER: No.

MAN: Why not?

SISTER: He'll say no.

MAN: God I hate this.

SISTER: What?

MAN: My bed's too big. I can't sleep. You think it's going to be nice to have all the space back but it's not. I just lie in the middle surrounded by this massive, king-sized confirmation of my loneliness.

SISTER: You can't sit around moping all evening.

MAN: I can.

SISTER: You shouldn't.

MAN: (*Standing.*) If someone doesn't kiss me in the next two minutes I'm going to die. One hundred and twenty – I'll count down – one hundred and eighteen, one hundred and seventeen…

SISTER: Mark!

MAN: I mean it, one hundred and fifteen.

SISTER: Can you count in your head please?

MAN: I can't cope with this.

SISTER: Sit down.

MAN: Somebody help me – I'm dying here.

SISTER: You're embarrassing me.

MAN: I feel like I'm going to explode…implode, something. Do you know how I feel? From loneliness.

SISTER: I haven't been kissed in a decade. That's not an
exaggeration.
MAN: (*Leaning down to her.*) Kiss me.

SISTER: What? Don't be stupid.
MAN: Kiss me.
SISTER: No.
MAN: Kiss me.
SISTER: Stop. Stop it.
MAN: Why not?
SISTER: You're my sister's –
MAN: No I'm not.
SISTER: No!
MAN: Please.
SISTER: Why are you doing this?
MAN: I think you're unique.
SISTER: Everyone's unique.
MAN: Kiss me.

SISTER: How long have I got to make up my mind?

MAN: Really?
SISTER: How long have I got?

MAN: I don't know, I just lost count.
SISTER: Great.
     (*She sits back in her chair.*)
MAN: Well?
SISTER: It's too late now, you've fucked it up.
MAN: Were you really going to kiss me?
SISTER: I'm not sure.
     (*He takes her hand over the table, she pulls it away.*)
     What are you doing?
MAN: I really like you.
SISTER: No you don't.
MAN: It's not because you remind me of your sister.
     (*She stands up.*
     He stands up.)

35

SISTER: I've got to go.
MAN: Don't go.
SISTER: It's late.
MAN: Take the pants.
SISTER: I'm not taking the pants.
MAN: Don't go.
SISTER: Don't…call me for a while.
MAN: I'm sorry.
SISTER: It's fine.
MAN: Tell your sister I love her.
SISTER: I won't.
MAN: I know.
>(*He leaves.*
>*She stays. She picks up the pants.*
>*The End.*)

Megan Walsh
LYRE

Characters

MOLLY, 22

MAX, 20

PAUL, 29

SUZY, 18

Lyre was first performed on 6 April 2007 as part of the HighTide Festival at The Cut in Halesworth, Suffolk, with the following company:

MOLLY, Hannah Taylor Gordon
MAX, Sam Hodges
PAUL, Gareth David-Lloyd
SUZY, Emily Gilchrist

Director Mary Nighy
Designers Josephine Callaghan
    Tanya Cunningham
Lighting Designer Lawrence Stromski
Sound Designer Steve Mayo
Composer Gustave André

SCENE ONE

*As the audience arrives, MOLLY is cleaning a harp, string by string. The
lighting is stark and casts shadows of the strings, like bars, across the stage.
There is a delicate rose/vine pattern on the sound board. It is hard for us
to see her face at certain angles and she occasionally wipes her brow from
the heat. A metronome ticks. Her brother MAX is asleep on a sofa.*

SCENE TWO

*MAX is smoking on the sofa, staring out at the audience. He is potentially
handsome, a little morose. The air is heavy with heat and his body is
slightly splayed to cool down. There is a fan pointed at him. He bites his
nails from time to time, looks at them and then returns to the audience.
The door clashes open on the chain. He leaps up, blows away the smoke
with the fan and lets MOLLY in. He walks to the other side of the room
and they face each other. MOLLY is wearing her mother's clothes – they
are large and too mature for her. She stands tall to compensate. She is
frenetic in countenance.*

MAX: I was just about to start. (*Beat.*) I was. (*Laughing nervously.*)
I was!

MOLLY: You mean to tell me you haven't done anything yet?

MAX: No I mean I'm just about to start again.

MOLLY: And what the hell d'you think you're doing smoking
in here?

MAX: I wasn't I was smoking it outside.

MOLLY: You'll smoke the wood and warp it.

MAX: So you say.

MOLLY: Spruce isn't normal wood Max. It's environmentally
sensitive. How many times do I have to tell you, you'll
make her pattern on the sound board fade, and how would
you feel then? How would you feel if it disappeared,
hm? And if that doesn't pluck any of your strings I'd also

like you to think about what all that smog is doing to your
synapses.

MAX: Oh God.

MOLLY: Exactly. They're shrivelling up like burnt hair. One
synapse per puff until it's too dark to think straight. And
then that's that. You're a light without a bulb.

MAX: (*Pause.*) What have you been reading?

MOLLY: Oh some article about identity and science. Very
interesting. You would have found it boring.

MAX: So why are you rattling on about it to me?
(*He settles down and becomes preoccupied with biting his nails
again.*)

MOLLY: What I was getting to was, I just want you to
know how glad I am that you're learning the harp.

MAX: You tell me that every day.

MOLLY: Because people who play musical instruments are
statistically more intelligent than people like me – who
don't. It'll keep you smart and it will help with your
blackouts. (*She steps away and brushes down her dress.*) I'll be
getting you on to Chinese next. Apparently it utilises both
hemispheres.

MAX: I don't want to learn Chinese.

MOLLY: Max?

MAX: Yeah.

MOLLY: How long have you been sitting there?

MAX: I'll do it in a minute Mol, can't you see I'm busy.

MOLLY: Have you even touched the strings today?

MAX: Yeah.

MOLLY: Are you lying again?

MAX: No.

MOLLY: Then why won't you look at me?
(*He smiles and looks at her.*)

MAX: You like me lying to you.
(*They hold a gaze.*)

MOLLY: No I don't.

MAX: You look nice.

MOLLY: Why don't you like what I'm wearing?
(*He looks her up and down and they hold each other's gaze.*)

MAX: I do.

MOLLY: You don't.

MAX: I've just seen that dress before.

MOLLY: So?

MAX: And it stinks.

MOLLY: That's impossible. I've washed it.

MAX: But you smell just like her. You smell of old lady – of compressed powder and ancient sweat.

MOLLY: I have to wear them for work.

MAX: No you don't.

MOLLY: Some of us have to work you know.

MAX: I think you should stop playing dress-up.

MOLLY: I'm not.

MAX: Take her clothes off.

MOLLY: No.

MAX: Leave them on then.

MOLLY: Why should I?

MAX: Up to you.

> (*Beat.*)

MOLLY: You really can smell it?

MAX: Yes.

MOLLY: And you're not lying?

MAX: No.

> (*Pause.*)

MOLLY: Fine.

> (*She pauses and then takes her clothes off down to her underwear, vest and tights, and stands looking at him, suddenly feeling more exposed.*)

Still there's no need to be so rude.

> (*He taps the sofa, ushering her to come and sit next to him. She goes and curls up with him on the sofa.*)

MAX: (*Tenderly.*) How is that woman you don't like at work?

MOLLY: Oh what Claudia? (*She sits up, animated and comfortable with her topic.*) She is such a nightmare. An ongoing nightmare. She never does the washing up but people don't care because she dresses for them, the boys. So guess who's left to do her dirty work?

MAX: Who?

43

MOLLY: Me. I think I'm going to poke the hornets' nest and
    I'm going to dob her in.

MAX: And say what?

MOLLY: That she doesn't do the washing up.

MAX: Why?

MOLLY: I don't know.

MAX: They'll just hate you.

MOLLY: Really?

MAX: Definitely.

MOLLY: Oh. So maybe I won't but Max?

MAX: In a minute.

MOLLY: You've got your grade four tomorrow and I think
    you're going to fail.

MAX: I'm gonna rinse it, don't worry.

MOLLY: But I am worried. (*Semi-lovingly.*) I pay for your
    lessons, I go to work and wear old clothes. I have to work
    extra for your lessons. It makes me happy to hear you
    play…

MAX: I don't care!

MOLLY: Oh.

MAX: Look I'm sorry. Okay? I'm grateful. Thank you. But
    Mol, why did it have to be the harp?

MOLLY: Don't start this now.

MAX: Of all instruments. In this area. I'm scared people can
    hear me. And I mean, look at my hands, they're, they're
    made for strangling lions, for ripping open watermelons,
    for (*He clenches them.*)

MOLLY: You have beautiful hands. You have the hands of
    a magician, or a watchmaker, or of an internationally
    acclaimed harpist. And look at that little finger – it's
    so long compared to the others

MAX: I don't use my little finger.

MOLLY: Well you should. Not many people have hands like
    that.
    (*MAX looks at his hands then bites his nails.*)
    Good. You need to keep them trim. Don't look at me like
    that.

MAX: It makes me odd.

MOLLY: You're not odd. You're a peacock.

MAX: I don't want to be a peacock.

MOLLY: No I know. You don't want to be anything at all. You want to be empty. But how many guys do you know who can play the harp as beautifully as you?

MAX: I don't know any guys who play the harp.

MOLLY: You know you could be in the local orchestra? Apparently they don't have a harpist and they're desperate. You wouldn't even have to try.

MAX: Why do you think I'm such a loser, Mol? I like a little competition – I just don't want to play that thing in front of anyone.

MOLLY: And do you know why? It's because you're one of life's flinchers – you don't actively want to do anything.

MAX: (*Desperate.*) I do I just don't like the one thing you're trying to make me do!
    (*MOLLY walks over to the harp.*)

MOLLY: I bet it's out of tune now. You've neglected her, look:
    (*She inspects. She plucks one sting. Then another. Then all of them.*)
    It's a good one you know. It deserves to be played.

MAX: I know but Mol. It's a harp. I'm a boy. And I like girls and stuff now.

MOLLY: You haven't got time to think about girls.

MAX: I think about them all the time.

MOLLY: Are you still lying about your 'girlfriend'?

MAX: No. (*Beat.*) Fine, my friends think I've got a girlfriend I'm trying to keep quiet.

MOLLY: And do you?

MAX: They think I'm going to meet her when I'm actually having lessons to play that girly instrument instead and I can't keep it up much longer.

MOLLY: So what's her name?

MAX: Who?

MOLLY: This imaginary floozie of yours.

MAX: That's the thing, I panicked, and I called her Sally. You see what a mess you've got me in?

MOLLY: Me?! I didn't do anything. (*Jealously.*) So why is she named after Mum?

MAX: It's the first name that comes into my head.

MOLLY: (*Still jealously.*) Why?

MAX: I don't know Mol, don't be like that.

MOLLY: No it's fine, I'm just surprised, that's all, that you pick her.

MAX: And it's got to the point where I should have done all sorts of shit with her now, you know, and obviously I haven't – because she's a harp. I'm running out of ideas Mol, I just want a girlfriend. That – that is my interest.

MOLLY: It better not be.

MAX: See you don't wanna listen.

MOLLY: Okay then. (*Beat.*) What's wrong with say, me?

MAX: Mol.

MOLLY: What?

MAX: Really?

MOLLY: Why not?

MAX: Are you teasing?

MOLLY: No.

MAX: That would be bad though.

MOLLY: Why?

MAX: Well, we'd have deformed kids and stuff
    (*Beat.*)

MOLLY: We wouldn't have kids you freak, we could just be living together. Like now. Just pretend. You know. Like when we were little, just pretend, haha, wouldn't that be funny!
    (*She tickles him and tries to make him laugh, but he laughs almost obligingly and then pushes her away.*)

MAX: Please don't.

MOLLY: You big spoil-sport, I was just trying to have a little fun. (*Beat.*) Fine, so tell me, what's stopping you getting a girl?

MAX: I need a guitar.

MOLLY: A harp is a guitar.

MAX: No it's not.

MOLLY: It used to be strummed with a plectrum.

MAX: Mol.

MOLLY: Without the lyre there'd be no guitar. You, my baby, are one step ahead of the game.

MAX: Yeah but I have to straddle this one like a stripper.

MOLLY: And you do it with such poise.

MAX: I want to sell it.

MOLLY: Max. It's the most precious thing we have left.
> (*He mouths the words as she says them.*)
> There's a memory in every string and every time I hear
> you play I can hear her playing too.
> (*He lies back exhausted and closes his eyes.*)
> And anyway, I think it's attractive to play the harp. (*Beat.*)
> Like…uh, you know, Apollo. Who was Apollo?

MAX: I don't care.

MOLLY: He was the Greek Adonis of music and what did he
> play?
> (*MAX shrugs.*)
> He played the lyre.

MAX: He didn't exist.

MOLLY: You shouldn't take the Lord's name in vain you little
> heathen now there's another word for lyre, do you know
> what it is? A cithara. It was also called a cithara, isn't that
> a beautiful word? (*Beat.*) Apollo did pretty well with the
> ladies you know.

MAX: He was a gaylord.

MOLLY: Apollo was popular with all the young people.

MAX: I'm not gay though am I?

MOLLY: I don't mind if you are.

MAX: Mum would've.

MOLLY: Are you?

MAX: No! This is exactly what I'm talking about. It warps stuff.
> This fucking thing. One minute I'm sitting here minding
> my own business, looking out of the window, having a
> think, and then in you come, you point at that and that's it,
> I'm a lazy gay nobody.

MOLLY: Well you're definitely lazy.
> (*Beat.*)

MAX: Leave me alone.

MOLLY: Fine.

MAX: And I gotta be up early tomorrow so don't you go
> waking me up polishing that damn thing.

MOLLY: Where are you going?

MAX: To work.

MOLLY: I thought we agreed that I'm the one who does that?

MAX: I've got a job. I'm going to be a lifeguard Mol. Girls like
lifeguards.

MOLLY: You're what?

MAX: I'm not such a bad swimmer and –
(*He lights a cigarette.*)

MOLLY: You better put that out before I do.
(*He puts out his cigarette.*)

MAX: Sorry.

SCENE THREE

*Swimming pool. PAUL, the chief lifeguard, swaggers on stage. There is
a girl, SUZY, loitering throughout the scene coquettishly. She unnerves
him.*

PAUL: Okay so no pushing, diving, running, ducking, no
under-eights in the jacuzzi, heavy petting is out of the
question – unless I'm involved get me? Long hair in caps
– makes the birds look bald but it's easier to spot the
fit ones, the lanes move anti-clockwise – not the norm,
but it's our policy – water slides haven't worked for four
months so if you see anyone trying to get up there, take the
motherfuckers down, now the wave machine comes on in
forty minute intervals but the under-fives tend to piss their
pants when the siren comes on so check that the chlorine
levels are strong enough to turn blond hair vert. Which
is French for green. Now, here's a list of all the kids who
should be wearing verucca socks, those things spread like
wildfire, I'm not fucking kidding you and if you see any of
these (*He points with disgust at the pool.*) floating in the water,
scoop 'em out because they don't conform to health and
safety.

MAX: What do I scoop them out with?

PAUL: Ah, we had a scooper somewhere… I usually just use
my hands, the filters push 'em to the side so it's dead easy.

MAX: Do you wear gloves for that?

PAUL: Being a lifeguard isn't about being a pussy Max Factor, it's about getting your hands wet.

MAX: It's just I have big hands. In case we need gloves. (*He holds them up.*)

PAUL: (*Squints.*) You've got girly hands mate. (*Pointing to the floating object.*) But they're big enough for that. Like I said we're mainly here to get crap out of the water now take this (*A whistle.*) and pop yourself up there.

(*MAX hesitantly climbs the lifeguard look-out and sits there. It is far too big for him and he looks exposed.*)

Right, now tell me what you see.

(*SUZY runs past in a swimming costume.*)

Whoah there, this is a non-running pool. There we go.

(*He watches her walk away, and she looks back at MAX.*)

Perks of the job mate. Right, now tell me what you see.

(*Pause.*) It's not a trick question, come on.

MAX: Water.

PAUL: Nice one Sherlock, now what do you really see?

(*Beat.*)

MAX: Er… (*He bites his bottom lip in stupidity.*)

PAUL: Right, hold it there. People plus water equals?

(*MAX looks at him blankly.*)

MAX: Swimming…pool?

PAUL: Remember the golden rule Factor Max? (*Beat.*) Water and people – don't mix. Which could mean people plus deep end, it could mean people plus paddling pool, it could mean drowning in Jacuzzi bubbles. (*He double takes and blows his whistle.*) Let go of his head. Yeah, you, no ducking! See what I mean? If I hadn't intervened then you might be doing a bit of bouche-à-bouche by now, yeah? Okay. So. What did I just say?

MAX: You said, that we –

PAUL: – don't want people drowning

MAX: No.

PAUL: So I want you to keep your eyes peeled for drowning.

MAX: Okay.

PAUL: What else, what else? (*He blows his whistle.*) Come on you two, it's not nice for other people when you do that in the pool. (*Back to MAX.*) Last week he was having it off with another bird. Lucky bastard. You got a girlfriend?

MAX: Yeah.

PAUL: Oh yeah? Didn't have you down as the type. Thought you might be gay.

MAX: I'm not.

PAUL: Doesn't bother me mate, you see all sorts being a lifeguard.

MAX: She's called Sally.

PAUL: Sally, Sally (*He goes through his mental rolodex.*) Sally what?

MAX: Er, Cithara.

PAUL: That Italian is it?

MAX: No like a lyre.

PAUL: You what?

MAX: A harp.

PAUL: Now that's a stupid fuckin' name. She from round here is she?

MAX: No.

PAUL: Thought not. She moved up here with you?

MAX: No.

PAUL: Why not?

MAX: I don't know.

PAUL: Gone off you?

MAX: Yeah.

PAUL: Happens mate. That why you're looking so fucking miserable?

MAX: Yeah.

PAUL: You should tell Sally whatsername you're a lifeguard now, fast-track it, tell her you're a capable, T-shirt-removable, shoulders-built-to-pack-a-swingable life-saver. Perk of the job mate.

MAX: But I'm not a lifeguard yet.

PAUL: Keep it down, thick shit. All you need is a high chair and a whistle and they fall for it. Seriously, she'll be putty. Free advice mate. That's all. Works a treat. (*He blows his whistle.*) Shower before entering the pool, yeah you.

KID'S VOICE: (*Offstage.*) Piss off you pervy wanker!

PAUL: What?! (*Blows his whistle.*) Right, that's it. (*As he's walking off.*) Little shit.

(*MAX looks around in a panic, marooned. He lowers his toe as if to dip it in water but pulls it back up afraid of the height. There is the faint sound of being underwater, blurred with the bustling sound of a swimming pool. He sits as he was in the first scene, biting his nails, his gaze adrift in the audience, but aware of SUZY's presence. He looks at his watch, wipes the palms of his hands on his shorts. He closes his eyes, opens them. SUZY approaches with a towel round her, which she drops a little and stands by his high chair.*)

SUZY: Hi.

MAX: (*Nervously.*) Hi.

SUZY: You look like a baby without a bib.

MAX: Oh right.

SUZY: Isn't that funny?

MAX: What?

SUZY: That you're supposed to be a lifeguard but you can't keep your eyes off me.

MAX: What?

SUZY: You shouldn't get so easily distracted.

(*Awkward silence. He gets out a packet of cigarettes and offers her one but she looks puzzled.*)

Can you do that here?

(*He lights the cigarette and tries to think of something to say while she, bemused, continues to gaze flirtatiously at him.*)

You're a very naughty boy aren't you?

MAX: (*Quietly.*) Uh I've got a girlfriend.

(*The surrounding sound of the pool starts to increase.*)

SUZY: What?

(*The noise starts to coagulate with the sound of being underwater.*)

MAX: I've er, I've got a girlfriend okay.

SUZY: What?!

MAX: I've got a girlfr....

PAUL: (*Shouts from just offstage.*) Wave machines going on, stand by!

(*Sirens begin for the wave machine. The sound of background noise of people gets louder, MAX panics and then plunges into the private sound of him sitting underwater. We can no longer hear anything else and the surrounding movements slow down. SUZY is talking to him, disgruntled that he's suddenly not paying her any attention, perhaps trying to play the coquette more overtly. PAUL comes back on stage, looks puzzled and then notices something in the pool. He blows his whistle although we can't hear it. SUZY starts to communicate with PAUL, looks around and in slow motion begins to look worried. She pulls on MAX's socks. PAUL and SUZY become more dismayed as MAX just sits there. PAUL edges frenetically around the side of the pool, removing his shoes and T-shirt in preparation for an heroic act. SUZY is shouting at MAX but he doesn't respond. Neither the audience nor MAX can hear her. Only the faint sound of harp strings can be heard. Blackout on PAUL taking a deep breath just as he's about to dive into the pool.*)

SCENE FOUR

A music examination waiting-room. MOLLY and MAX are sitting in silence waiting for his exam. MOLLY is in the same clothes as in Scene Two. The harp is sitting at a jaunty angle to the stage; it casts a large shadow, as in the first scene. There is the sound of someone hammering away at the piano.

MOLLY: Right you (*Pursing her lips and pointing her finger.*) I don't want to hear another word! Is that clear?
(*Pause as they listen to the paino music offstage. There is an awkward moment which she decides to break with a chirpy change of tone.*)
Ah we've got a right show-off in there, haven't we? I bet half of those trills aren't in the music, he's just fluffing it up for the examiner. (*She looks around and straightens her dress.*) Maybe you should fluff it up a little, eh?
(*She gets up and opens the door ever so slightly to look in on the kid playing the piano. MAX ushers her away from the door but she motions to him to be quiet. The loud music leaks into the waiting-room. She closes the door and sits down.*)

What you see when you haven't got a gun.

MAX: Eh?

MOLLY: I mean how old do you reckon he is?

MAX: Who?

MOLLY: Little Mozart in there.

MAX: I don't know.

MOLLY: Guess. (*Pause.*) Bet you can't. Come on it's fun.

MAX: Sixteen.

MOLLY: Nope!

MAX: My age.

MOLLY: Nope!

MAX: Oo let me think, some little two year-old piano prodigy.

MOLLY: Well you're not completely wrong, I don't reckon he
could be more than seven.

MAX: Well good for him.

MOLLY: Honestly, you've never seen anything like it. He
holds his hands like tripods, like this, you know, like he's
plugging the keyboard or like his fingers are...

MAX: Keep your voice down.

MOLLY: (*In a lower hush but animatedly as if trying to tell an
interesting story.*) And he's got his head resting back on his
neck with his eyes squeezed shut in a kind of 'I'm so lost
in this music' kind of way and I'll tell you something, I
think it looks so ridiculous. (*Pause.*) It's the parents' fault
of course. No excuse for that kind of thing, bringing up
a child thinking he's the queen bee born to make sweet
music his whole life when you and I both know he's just a
drone. A machine. He's not a patch on you...

MAX: Why do you have to be like that?

MOLLY: God knows what he'll be like in a couple a years. No
thanks. (*Pause.*) Oh well. (*Beat.*) They start so young these
days don't they?

MAX: Are we talking about sex again?

MOLLY: (*Desperately.*) How can you compete with that?

MAX: I don't want to.

MOLLY: See, that's always been the problem. No fighting
spirit. You need to give life a bit of welly, a bit of muscle.

Anyway, I didn't mean just you, I meant everyone. Me too. All of us on the shelf.

MAX: What shelf?

MOLLY: If I'd learnt the piano as soon as I could walk I'd be as good as that little kid in there. (*She looks at her watch.*) You got everything ready? (*Pause.*) Are you listening to me?

MAX: Yeah. (*He hunches his shoulders and looks away.*)

MOLLY: Now listen here. I don't want to have to go over this again so I'm only going to say it one more time, okay? You listening?

MAX: Yeah.

MOLLY: No one drowned did they?

MAX: No.

MOLLY: So what's the problem?

MAX: She almost did.

MOLLY: But she didn't did she?

MAX: No.

MOLLY: So what the hell are you still worried about? It wasn't your fault, was it? You're not a lifeguard. You're a musician, remember, you play the harp, you're not a, you're not a, look at you, you couldn't save a piece of paper from a puddle, and off you went to live out your Baywatch fantasy.

MAX: I didn't.

MOLLY: I told you that job was a mindless idea, listen to me more carefully in the future. You nearly cost us everything we've worked for so you better make up for it when you go in there because you owe it to me. You're gonna focus on what you've got to do in there. You're gonna roll your fingers over those strings like you've never rolled them before – and you're not going to pluck them like the clunking useless piece of crap you've been over the last couple of days. Keep your elbows low, your wrists fluid – don't tense your wrists, same goes for your back, shoulders and neck. Go soft on the pedals for the key changes and make sure you roar up and down the strings for the glissando rather than limping through it. And whatever you do, make sure every note is an expression of how much you love the music, make it mean something again. Because this is what we've been working on. This is what you're here for. So give 'em hell. And make sure you smile at the examiner. And remember your posture. Sit up, come on. You've got to look ready. Are you ready?

MAX: Yes.

MOLLY: Need some water?

MAX: Thanks. (*He takes her bottle and drinks the whole thing.*)

MOLLY: You're gonna need the loo now. Go on you better go.
(*The music in the background finally comes to a stop.*)
No, too late. Get back here. Thank god that racket's stopped, it was starting to make my blood boil. Now do you need a hand moving it in or anything?

MAX: No just promise me you won't listen.

MOLLY: Oh come on, don't go all shy on me I've heard you play a thousand times, you know I love to hear you play.

MAX: I won't go in unless you go away.

MOLLY: Fine. I'll be in the car park. Give me a call when you're out. Keep your head up. Oh God, you haven't taped your fingers.

MAX: I don't need to.

MOLLY: See, there's all the proof I need – they should be bleeding and swollen with over-use.

MAX: I'll give you a call when I'm out.

MOLLY: Good luck, remember to smile, enjoy it, I would have given anything to be able to do what you can, just let it all flow out and give 'em hell, okay?
(*MAX opens the door, checks it's okay to go in and then wheels away the harp. MOLLY waits and then sits down again, biting her nails and looking at her watch. Harp music begins to be heard offstage. It is actually quite good, but mustn't sound too polished. She creeps up to the door and listens through the crack, hesitates and creeps away backwards. She sits down again. The music sounds good. She stares out at the audience, then smells her dress and dabs her eyes with it and then rests her head back, eyes closed. Blackout.*)

SCENE FIVE

The harp sits destroyed in the living-room. The strings are curled and splayed, the main body has been crushed. It lies on its side. A faint spot enables the audience to see it. A light is turned on outside/offstage, and moments later MOLLY walks in. She turns on the light. MAX is sitting in the corner but she doesn't notice him. There is a metronome ticking in the background for the duration of the scene but faint enough so as not to be annoying. There is a scar on his nose.

MAX: Mol? (*Pause.*) Hey, Mol? (*Beat.*) I'm here.

(*MOLLY turns around to look at him cowering in the corner.*)

Can you turn the metronome off Mol? It's making me angry.

(*She pauses and looks at him in horror but gathers some composure.*)

MOLLY: Oh baby have you been waiting for me all this time? I'm so sorry I'm late, it's just why don't you open a window it's stiflingly hot in here isn't it?

MAX: No.

MOLLY: Huh? Oh, uh, you know look, I'm sorry, Claudia, she was at it again, you know, and turn the metronome off please it's driving me mad where was I?

(*She stands up tall and refuses to make eye contact with the harp at the front of the stage.*)

You look ill. What have you been eating are you ill?

MAX: No I'm feeling better.

MOLLY: Oh really?

MAX: Yeah, I destroyed the harp.

MOLLY: Because I brought home some fish for dinner, because it's brain food. It uh, helps with synapse growth and your memory.

MAX: Did you hear what I just said?

MOLLY: It's so you can remember all your fingerwork and you can play it just the way Mum did and we can remember the good old days, eh?

MAX: But we don't have a harp anymore.

MOLLY: Because we need to remember her now she's gone

MAX: I don't want to remember anymore. (*He lights a cigarette.*)

MOLLY: And you can put that fucking thing out. Not in here you hear me? Not in here next to the...

MAX: Next to the what?

MOLLY: To the harp.

MAX: But look. (*He stands up.*) It doesn't work Molly, or have you gone out of your mind? Look. I cut the strings myself. I cut the black ones and then the oranges and then the dirty old white ones. I even had to go out and get some hedge clippers to prune the lower register – they're tough old gut and don't go without a fight... There's a lot of tension in those strings isn't there Mol?

MOLLY: Yeah. (*Tentatively, as if trying to teach him.*) And do you know how much tension there is?

MAX: No Molly I don't.

MOLLY: The tension of the strings on the sound board is equal to a ton.

MAX: See that makes perfect sense to me cos they didn't go without a fight, look (*Points to the scar on his nose.*) the C3 leapt up and bit me on the snout, she wasn't gonna go without lashing me first.

MOLLY: Well I hope it scars.

MAX: And I bet you're thinking that I deserved it but I didn't want to take any chances Mol, so I crushed the sound board too, it's dead easy to break, if you really put some welly into it, give it a bit of muscle.

MOLLY: You can be quiet now.

(*She walks over to it but stands away to look, as if it were a dead body. She moves gently towards it and tries to make it stand up, but it won't. She then tries to pull it to the edge of the stage.*)

MAX: What are you doing?

MOLLY: I'm getting it out of the way.

MAX: It's not a car accident, we're not creating a jam. Leave it be. It should stay right there.

(*She keeps pushing the harp over to the side of the room, using the strings to pull it.*)

MOLLY: Can you turn the metronome off please?

MAX: In a minute.

MOLLY: It's going to take weeks to fix this.

MAX: It's not going to be fixed.

MOLLY: No because it would take a time machine to mend this, one that could take me all the way back to the moment before you smashed it to pieces so that I'd have enough time to go into the kitchen pick up a frying-pan and wait in the corner while you loped about, wondering which string you were going to cut first. And just before you did, I'd come down on you so hard you'd be out cold like you might not wake up again. And then I'd be the one in trouble for a change. But at least I wouldn't have to look at this and feel what I'm feeling now. I wouldn't be wondering why you had to go and do it and break my har–

MAX: (*Mockingly.*) My God Mol, a frying-pan? You want to kill me with a frying-pan? You can be really out of line sometimes you know that? At least do it with something sharp for a change.

(*He puts on his coat. He starts to look at himself in the mirror, arranging his collar, and she looks at him in horror.*)

MOLLY: Where are you going?

(*He ignores her and continues to preen.*)

Wait! I'm sorry! Wait. You're right. Just give me a moment to get things right.

(*She stands there and starts to unbutton her dress.*)

Max?

MAX: What are you doing?

MOLLY: I just thought you'd prefer me without them on?

MAX: I don't care either way just get changed somewhere else, have a little dignity why don't you.

MOLLY: Oh.

(*She scrambles to do them back up again. She goes to sit on the sofa and pats it to tempt him over.*)

MAX: And I know what I've done, so you don't have to spell it out for me. I'm not sorry.

MOLLY: Oh now come on, you're just playing up now, come on, come and sit by me.

MAX: No.

MOLLY: No?

MAX: No.

MOLLY: Why?

MAX: Why not?

MOLLY: You're being petulant.

MAX: I might go out.

MOLLY: You better not.

MAX: I might.

MOLLY: When will you be home?

MAX: Not sure.

MOLLY: Do you want some dinner first, I got a lovely bit of fish.

MAX: No thanks.

(*Pause.*)

MOLLY: What do I have left?

(*Pause.*)

MAX: You have me.

MOLLY: Because, you were getting so much better – you got a merit without even practising.

(*He lights a cigarette and begins to smoke it defiantly.*)

MAX: (*After a couple of drags.*) I think I'm gonna smoke this outside.

(*He leaves.*
Blackout.)

SCENE SIX

MOLLY is polishing the broken but now semi-fixed harp. MAX is not there.

The End.

Sam Holcroft
NED & SHARON

Characters

SHARON, 16

GRAEME, 25

NED, 18

Ned & Sharon was first performed on 6 April 2007 as part of the HighTide Festival at The Cut in Halesworth, Suffolk, with the following company:

SHARON, Charlie Covell
GRAEME, Hywel John
NED, Adam Lake

Director Anne Tipton
Designers Josephine Callaghan
            Tanya Cunningham
Lighting Designer Lawrence Stromski
Sound Designer Steve Mayo

SCENE ONE

SHARON's bedroom in a residential care home for minors awaiting foster care or return to their families.

SHARON sits on the sofa watching porn. The TV screen cannot be seen but the noises can be heard.

The door opens. GRAEME, a care assistant, steps in.

GRAEME: Please turn it off Sharon.

> (*Beat.*)
> Please turn if off now.
> (*Beat.*
> *GRAEME moves into the room and kneels down by the television to switch it off.*)

SHARON: Wait.

> (*GRAEME stops.*)
> Give it a second.
> (*GRAEME turns back to the TV. The come shot. They watch, entranced.*
> *GRAEME snaps it off.*)
> Good huh?

GRAEME: Where did you get this?

> (*SHARON shrugs.*)
> Please tell me where you got this Sharon?
> (*GRAEME ejects the video and stands up.*)
> I don't want to have to place more restrictions on you.
> (*Beat.*)
> Well then. I'm going to take away your internet privileges.

SHARON: You're a cunt.

GRAEME: And two points.

SHARON: Fuck you.

GRAEME: Three points.

> (*GRAEME moves to the door.*)

SHARON: Where are you going with that?

GRAEME: Confiscating it.

SHARON: *Confiscating it!* You're taking it back to your fucking room.

GRAEME: Please don't speak to me like that.

SHARON: You're going to wank over it aren't you? You're going to fill your lap with come over that.

GRAEME: I'm not talking to you when you're like this.
(*He moves out.*)

SHARON: Give me back my video you stealing fuck!

GRAEME: Don't shout at me, please. I'm *confiscating* your video.

SHARON: (*Shouts out into the corridor.*) You're stealing my fucking porn to wank over because you're a lonely fuck!
(*GRAEME darts back into the room.*)

GRAEME: Keep your voice down.

SHARON: You're stealing my porn!

GRAEME: I'm not stealing your porn.

SHARON: You are stealing my porn to wank over!

GRAEME: For God's sake, I've got my own porn, haven't I?

SHARON: Have you? Have you got your own porn?

GRAEME: Sharon that's enough!

SHARON: Are you shouting at me?

GRAEME: No, Sharon.

SHARON: I think you were.

GRAEME: I'm sorry. I'm sorry I shouted Sharon. That was the wrong thing to do. I'm going to leave now.

SHARON: Give me back my video!

GRAEME: Enough Sharon. You know the rules.

SHARON: I paid for that with my own money.

GRAEME: No Sharon.

SHARON: Fuck!
(*SHARON swipes a shelf clear of things.*)

GRAEME: Clear it up.

SHARON: Give it back.

GRAEME: No Sharon, you are not getting it back.

SHARON: (*Explodes.*) Fuck! I hate you!

GRAEME: I can go and get Leanne.

SHARON: I fucking HATE Leanne!

GRAEME: Sharon.

SHARON: Fucking shit. Shit place is doing my head in. You're all fucks!

GRAEME: It's alright Sharon.

(*SHARON grabs a large bottle of Coca-Cola and starts to shake it up.*)

Sharon put that down.

(*She shakes it until it is all frothy inside.*)

Sharon. Don't.

SHARON: Give me back my video.

GRAEME: No.

(*Beat.*

GRAEME darts to snatch the bottle but she ducks away, unscrews the cap and sprays Coca-Cola all over him and her room.

GRAEME stands dripping.

He walks out.

SHARON stands looking at the mess.

A minute later GRAEME enters with NED, a janitor, holding a mop and bucket filled with soapy water.)

SHARON: Who are you?

GRAEME: This is Ned. He's new.

(*NED starts mopping.*)

Ned, don't do that.

(*NED stops.*)

Sharon's going to do that.

SHARON: Fuck off.

GRAEME: This is your mess.

SHARON: I can see your nipples.

(*GRAEME looks down at his wet T-shirt.*)

GRAEME: I'm going to change my T-shirt. Sharon you clean up your mess. I won't be a minute.

(*GRAEME goes.*

SHARON and NED stand still for a minute.)

SHARON: I fizzed up the coke. I shook it all up and fizzed it right in his face.

That's bad, right?

(*NED shrugs.*)

I didn't mean to. Fuck it!

(*She jabs the sofa.*)

He's going to take away my internet privileges. I've gone
and totally fucked it now. Fuck.

NED: It's not that bad.

SHARON: No?

NED: No. If you clean it up, they won't be so hard on you.

SHARON: You think?

NED: Yeah.

SHARON: Think they'll let me use the internet?

(*NED shrugs.*)

NED: Never know.

(*He holds out the mop for her.*
She takes it.)

You put it in the bucket, then squeeze it in there –

SHARON: I know.

(*SHARON dunks the mop in the bucket and lifts it out.*)

NED: You've got to squeeze it in there –

SHARON: Alright.

NED: Otherwise it makes a mess.

SHARON: I already made a mess.

NED: More mess.

(*SHARON squeezes it out and starts to mop the floor.*
GRAEME enters.)

GRAEME: Well done Sharon.

SHARON: See, I cleaned it up.

GRAEME: That's good Sharon. Well done.

(*SHARON looks to NED and smiles.*
She turns back to GRAEME.)

SHARON: Can I use the internet then?

GRAEME: No.

SHARON: What?

GRAEME: Sharon if you behave like that you have to face the
consequences –

SHARON: Fuck's sake!

GRAEME: Sharon.

(*SHARON throws the mop down.*)

Sharon!

(*NED goes to pick up the mop.*)

GRAEME: Leave it Ned.

(*Beat.*)

Pick that up Sharon.

(*Beat.*)

Pick that up and give it back to Ned.

(*SHARON doesn't move.*)

Ned used to live here. He used to live here just like you. He used to break the rules and he'd have his privileges taken away from him until he learned to behave. And you know what? He started listening, he changed his behaviour, and when he was old enough he went in to the Aftercare programme and we helped him get his own place, (*To NED.*) isn't that right? You have your own home; you make your own rules now. And he's got this job, making his own money. You could learn a thing or two from Ned.

(*SHARON looks at NED.*)

SHARON: You used to live here?

(*NED nods.*

Beat.

SHARON bends down and picks up the mop. She hands it back to NED.)

NED: Thanks.

GRAEME: Alright Ned. You can go.

(*NED goes out. SHARON watches him go.*)

Sharon? I got you a new video.

SCENE TWO

SHARON is watching a video: 'A Bug's Life'. She is eating a bag of crisps. When she is finished she scrunches up the bag and throws it against the wall; GRAEME comes in just at that moment with her supper tray.

GRAEME: Please pick that up Sharon.

SHARON: What is this video?

GRAEME: Sharon.

SHARON: A fucking bug's circus? What am I? Fucking five?

GRAEME: Sharon you don't need to swear.

SHARON: Fuck.

GRAEME: I have to take two points Sharon.

SHARON: You think I'm stupid?

GRAEME: No, that's not what I think.

SHARON: Fucking cartoons. I'm sixteen!

(*She gets up off the sofa.*)

I'm getting another one.

GRAEME: Please sit down Sharon. Sharon! You know that you have to have your supper in here because of the way you behaved today. You are being separated from the group. Please sit down.

(*SHARON slides back down.*)

Thank you.

You've got shepherd's pie with green beans.

(*He places the tray beside her.*)

SHARON: What's that?

GRAEME: Sponge pudding.

SHARON: Looks rank.

(*He takes the pudding off the tray.*)

Where are you going with my pudding?

GRAEME: If you're going to be like that about your food, then you won't have it.

SHARON: No, you just want it for yourself. Like my video.

(*GRAEME turns to go.*)

You're going to watch my video, eat my pudding, rub your dick.

(*GRAEME walks to the door.*)

Maybe you'll just stick your dick in my pudding.

(*GRAEME goes.*)

Give me back my pudding!

(*SHARON slams the side of the tray sending her shepherd's pie flying.*

GRAEME comes back to the door, sees the pie and disappears again.

A minute later he arrives back with NED and his mop and bucket.)

Hi Ned.

GRAEME: Clean it up Sharon, I don't want any fuss. I've had just about enough of you today.

(*GRAEME goes.*)

SHARON: I did it again.

(*NED looks at the mess.*)

Probably lose ten points. Back down to level one.

I have to eat my food in my room.

(*Beat.*)

I didn't want my dinner anyway.

NED: You won't be saying that later when you're hungry.

SHARON: I don't care. I'm fat anyway.

NED: No you're not.

SHARON: What about all this?

NED: It's not fat. It's normal.

SHARON: You think so?

NED: Yeah.

(*Beat.*)

If you clean it up they'll give you another one.

SHARON: No they won't.

NED: Yes they will. They don't want you going hungry.

SHARON: They don't?

NED: No. They don't want to be done for starving you.

SHARON: They fucking get to me.

NED: You just got to learn how to work them, that's all.

(*He hands her some kitchen towel. She gets down to scoop up her dinner. NED helps her.*)

SHARON: You're not supposed to help me.

NED: I know.

(*They scoop up the pie together.*)

SHARON: So what movies d'you like?

NED: I don't know.

(*NED shrugs.*)

D'you like Batman?

Batman movies?

NED: Yeah I guess.

SHARON: I love them. My favourite's 'Batman Begins'. The new one. It's not like the others is it? It's like a real movie. I saw it at the cinema, did you?

NED: Yeah, it's good.

SHARON: But I can't watch it here because it's only on DVD and I don't have DVD. D'you?

NED: No.

SHARON: Oh.

NED: My mate Tony has a DVD player.

SHARON: Does he?

NED: Yeah. So I get to watch it round his.

SHARON: Does he have it?

NED: He's got everything.

SHARON: Everything?

NED: Most things, yeah.

SHARON: Wow. That's nice. That you can go round your friend's and watch DVDs.

NED: Yeah. It is.

SHARON: Do you have a girlfriend?

NED: No.

SHARON: Do you want one?

(*GRAEME comes in and sees them close together on the floor.*)

GRAEME: Ned please don't help her. This is her mess to clean up.

(*NED stands up and moves away.*)

Come on Sharon; don't think that Ned hasn't got better things to do than wait around for you.

(*SHARON mops hurriedly. She hands the mop back to NED.*)

SHARON: Sorry I didn't mean to keep you waiting.

(*NED takes the mop and goes out.*)

SCENE THREE

SHARON sits on her bed thinking. She gets up decidedly and goes to the mirror to adjust her hair. She takes a bottle of squash on the side, unscrews the cap and empties it onto the floor.
She opens the door and peers out into the hallway.

SHARON: Graeme.

   GRAEME.

   (*GRAEME comes in.*)

GRAEME: Sharon please don't shout. People don't want to hear you shouting down the corridor.

   (*He sees the squash all over the floor.*)

   We can keep doing this for as long as you want, it's no skin off my nose. As long as you make a mess, you can clean it up.

(*GRAEME goes out. SHARON grins.*)
(*GRAEME comes back with a mop and bucket. SHARON waits for NED to follow. He doesn't.*)

SHARON: Where's Ned?

GRAEME: He's busy.

SHARON: Why?

GRAEME: He has a job to do. It doesn't involve waiting around for you.

SHARON: But I want to see him.

GRAEME: He's working. You've got to clean up this mess.

SHARON: But I want to see him!

GRAEME: Clean it up, Sharon.

(*GRAEME goes.*)

SHARON: Graeme. Graeme!

(*GRAEME comes back.*)

GRAEME: He's not coming, Sharon.

This is not a joke. If you want to be treated like a grown-up then please start acting like one. Clean this up.

(*GRAEME goes.*

SHARON looks at the mess forlornly. She takes the mop and starts slapping the juice with it. She slaps the floor with the mop over and over; she kicks over the bucket and spills the soapy water. When she is finished she turns the bucket upright and begins to clean up the mess.)

SCENE FOUR

SHARON paces around her room. She opens the door.

SHARON: (*Whispers.*) Graeme. *Graeme.*

(*GRAEME comes in.*)

GRAEME: What is it?

SHARON: See, I didn't shout?

GRAEME: That's good. What is it, Sharon?

SHARON: It's about Ned.

GRAEME: What about Ned?

SHARON: I want to see him.

GRAEME: He's working Sharon.

SHARON: After he's finished working.

GRAEME: Then he goes home.

SHARON: Well before he goes home. Could you ask him if he wants to watch a video? When he's finished? D'you think you could ask him? Please.

(*Beat.*)

GRAEME: I don't think so Sharon.

SHARON: Just to watch a video. Just ask him.

GRAEME: I don't know Sharon.

SHARON: I didn't spill nothing. Look. I didn't throw nothing on the floor for two days. I've been good. I only lost two points, and that's only because I couldn't swallow my vitamin and it looked like I spat it out at her, but I didn't. But I didn't spill nothing, for two days. And you said that if I behaved like a grown-up then you'd treat me like one. So. Will you ask him for me?

(*Beat.*)

GRAEME: Alright, I'll ask, only because you've been so good. But he might say no, Sharon.

SHARON: I don't care.

GRAEME: Are you sure? You're not going to get angry if he says no?

SHARON: No. I promise.

GRAEME: Then because you've made me a promise I'll take your word for it, alright?

SHARON: Yeah.

GRAEME: Okay.

SHARON: Thanks Graeme.

GRAEME: That's alright.

(*GRAEME goes.*)

SHARON: Graeme?

(*GRAEME stops.*)

Are you going to ask him now?

GRAEME: Right now?

SHARON: Yeah.

GRAEME: Alright I'll go find him.

SHARON: And you come straight back here and tell me?

GRAEME: Alright.

SHARON: Thanks.

GRAEME: That's okay.

(*GRAEME goes.*
SHARON paces around her room.
GRAEME comes back in.)

GRAEME: I found him down the hall.

SHARON: What did he say?

GRAEME: He'll watch a video with you.

SHARON: He will?

GRAEME: Yes.

SHARON: Oh right.

GRAEME: He gets off at six so he'll come to a watch a video
then. Alright?
But Sharon I'm trusting you. I'm trusting you not to break
any rules okay. I'm trusting you to behave responsibly. I
don't want to regret this.

SHARON: You won't. You won't regret it. I'll be good as gold.
I promise.

GRAEME: Alright then. What would you like to watch?

SHARON: Batman.

SCENE FIVE

SHARON is getting ready in her room. She is nervous.
The door opens. GRAEME and NED enter.

SHARON: Hi Ned.

NED: Hi Sharon.

GRAEME: So you guys are going to watch a video then?

SHARON: Yeah. (*To NED.*) I got some videos, you can choose
what you want to watch I've seen them all before.

GRAEME: Okay, I'll leave you guys to it, but I'll be just down
the hall. I'm just down the hall, okay?
(*GRAEME goes out closing the door behind him.*)

SHARON: I got a selection, d'you want to choose? Cos I've
seen them all before, so you can just choose whichever one
you want.
(*NED comes down to the TV and looks through the videos.*)
Which one do you want?

NED: I don't really mind.

SHARON: Do you like any of them? We can get some different
ones, I'll get Graeme and he can get us some different
ones?

NED: No they're all really good.

SHARON: Yeah?

NED: Yeah.

SHARON: Well which one do you want to watch – shall we
watch Batman?

NED: Yeah, alright.

SHARON: Okay.

(*SHARON takes the Batman video out of its case and inserts it
into the video player. NED sits on the sofa to watch. SHARON
comes and sits beside him.*)

I'm glad you wanted to watch a video. I was really
nervous. I thought you'd say no.

NED: No.

SHARON: I was worried you would.

NED: No, I wanted to…watch a video.

SHARON: I didn't know what to wear.

NED: It's nice.

SHARON: It is?

NED: Yeah.

SHARON: I don't know.

NED: You look nice.

SHARON: Thanks. You look nice.

(*NED blushes.*
NED looks away.
They both settle down into the sofa.
The video plays.
NED reaches out and takes SHARON's hand.)

SCENE SIX

SHARON tidies her room.
GRAEME comes in.

GRAEME: Well this is a first. Well done Sharon, five points.

SHARON: Five?

GRAEME: Yes definitely. You've been good all day. I'm very impressed. Soon you'll be back up to level two and we can reinstate your full leisure time. Start thinking about what you'd like to do.

SHARON: I want to do sports. Cos I'm fat.

GRAEME: Um.

SHARON: Where's Ned?

GRAEME: He left.

SHARON: What?

GRAEME: He didn't say, but it seemed like it was important, because he left straight after his shift.

SHARON: But we're supposed to be watching a video.

GRAEME: I know.

I'm sure it was important.

SHARON: Does he not want to watch a video with me?

GRAEME: I'm sure he… He's probably busy. Why don't you watch one anyway?

SHARON: I don't want to watch a video on my own.

GRAEME: Sure you do.

SHARON: Why the fuck would I want to watch one on my own! I don't want to be on my own.

GRAEME: There's no need to shout.

SHARON: I'm not fucking shouting!

GRAEME: Why don't I sit with you?

SHARON: Don't be fucking funny.

GRAEME: I'm not.

SHARON: I don't want to watch a video with *you*.

(*She paces around the room. She is deeply upset.*)

GRAEME: Sharon it's alright.

SHARON: No it's not. We had a really good time. I really had a good time.

(*She knocks some things onto the floor.*)

GRAEME: Sharon.

(*She knocks some more things.*)

Please don't do that.

You've been doing so well. Please don't spoil it.

You're so nearly at level two.

SHARON: Fuck level two!

(*She thumps her fists against the wall and kicks the bin across the floor.*)

GRAEME: Sharon!

(*She picks up a jug of drink that was for them to share.*)

Sharon don't. He's not here to clean it up.

SHARON: Why?

(*She is about to drop the jug when NED appears in the doorway.*)

NED: Hi Sharon.

(*He is carrying a DVD player under his arm and a copy of 'Batman Begins' on DVD.*)

Sorry I'm late. I went round to Tony's to get his DVD, so we could watch 'Batman Begins'. If you want to?

SHARON: I love 'Batman Begins'!

NED: I know. That's why I got it.

SHARON: But d'you know how to plug that in? You've got to have the right leads?

NED: I've got them.

SHARON: You have?

NED: Yeah.

SHARON: Where?

NED: Here.

(*GRAEME is forgotten. They come down to the TV together. GRAEME watches for a moment before going out, closing the door behind him.*)

SHARON: Cos I don't know how to do it.

(*They both get down on their knees and inspect the television.*)

NED: I know how to do it.

SHARON: Do you?

(*He hands her the lead with the plug.*)

NED: You need to plug that into the socket.

(*She takes it to the socket.*)

But not yet! We should hook it up first or you might get a shock.

SHARON: Okay. What about this one?

NED: This one goes into the back of the DVD and then into the TV, see? Like that.

SHARON: I thought you weren't going to come.

NED: Why?

(*SHARON shrugs.*)

SHARON: (*About the DVD cord.*) Is it the right way round?

NED: Yeah, I think so.

I wanted to come.

Pass me the remote.

(*SHARON passes him the remote control.*)

SHARON: That's for the TV.

NED: Yeah, I need both.

(*He inspects both the TV remote and the DVD remote.*)

SHARON: I thought you wasn't coming.

I shouted at Graeme.

I made that mess.

(*NED looks around at the mess on the floor.*)

NED: Why d'you do that Sharon?

SHARON: I thought you wasn't going to come.

NED: I was always going to come, Sharon.

SHARON: Yeah but I didn't know that.

(*Beat.*)

NED: You've got to take it easy on yourself Sharon. I had a good time with you.

(*SHARON falls silent. NED carries on hooking up the DVD player. SHARON gets up and puts all the clutter back on the shelves. She comes back down to NED. He smiles at her and hands her the cord to plug into the wall. She inserts it and the machine springs to life.*)

SHARON: It's working!

NED: Told you.

(*SHARON grabs his arm.*
NED reddens.)

Give us the DVD.

(*She hands him the DVD and he inserts it into the player and turns on the TV.*)

Go on then, sit down.

SHARON: Is it working?

NED: Yeah, go and sit down.

(*SHARON goes and sits on the sofa. NED comes and sits beside her. They settle down.*)

SHARON: Ned?

NED: Yeah.

SHARON: Do you think, when it's finished, and you go after, do you think we can have a goodnight kiss.

NED: I…I don't know.

SHARON: We won't be breaking the rules. I can ask Graeme if we're allowed. Shall I ask him? I'll go and ask him.

(*She gets up off the sofa and heads for the door.*)

Stop the video, I mean DVD. Stop the DVD until I come back. Can you stop it?

NED: Yeah.

(*NED pauses the DVD. SHARON goes out. NED stays on the sofa, he looks worried.*

After a while SHARON comes back in.)

SHARON: Yeah he said we can. Because I asked. He said we can have a goodnight kiss. If we want.

(*She comes back and sits on the sofa.*)

So we can have a kiss when you go.

Play the video, I mean DVD.

(*NED presses play on the remote. 'Batman Begins'…*)

Do you want to wait until you go?

NED: I don't mind.

SHARON: We could have a kiss now, *and* when you go.

(*Beat.*)

Do you want to?

NED: Alright.

SHARON: Okay.

(*They lean in and kiss. The kiss grows and they become locked together. After a while they disengage, stand and move towards the bed. They lie down together and kiss again.*

The door opens and GRAEME looks in. He sees them on the bed. The pair freeze.

Silence.

GRAEME quickly steps back into the corridor and closes the door.

NED and SHARON sit up.)

NED: Should we watch the DVD then?

SHARON: Yeah.

Yeah.

(*They get up and come back to the sofa.*)

Rewind it then, can you rewind it?

NED: Yeah.

(*They settle on the sofa.*
NED stops and starts the DVD. and 'Batman Begins' begins
again...)

SCENE SEVEN

It's late at night. GRAEME is on the phone.

GRAEME: Well, no actually. She seems calmer. She seems to be
more at peace. When she's with him. She seems in control,
involved, attentive maybe. And her points, well she's way
into level two and climbing.

(*Beat.*)

I know that but the system is based on reward; good
behaviour is rewarded with increasing levels of
independence. But she doesn't seem to value that as much
as company. She doesn't like to be alone. Her history. She
was left alone. And she responds well to company, she
behaves, given that reward.

(*Beat.*)

No. I'm not suggesting that he is a reward. I didn't intend
to encourage that kind of...friendship, of course not. But
she, as I said, is...happy.

(*Beat.*)

Yes. Yes I know. When he didn't come on time, yes. And
she thought he wouldn't come at all. Yes, she did go into
one of her rages and nearly broke a hole in the wall.
Kicked the bin. But he did come. He did come, eventually.

(*Beat.*)

No, I appreciate that's not the point. But –

(*Beat.*)

Yes, our policy, I wanted to be clear on that, that's why I
called –

(*Beat.*)

Yes I was briefed but –

(*Beat.*)

No. I mean yes. Yes I did say she could kiss him. But it was
just a goodnight kiss, that's all I said, I didn't expect –
(*Beat.*)
No as I said I would never intend to encourage that kind
of… But –
(*Beat.*)
No, I'm not bending the rules for her. I'm not trying to
suggest that it's okay in this situation. I don't think. No. No
it's just that. It's just that she, her self-esteem, with him…
(*Beat.*)
Exactly. I'm well aware that Sharon's situation here is
fragile. And that she may not ever be able to return
home, and that's why, well, that's why this…friendship is
important –
(*Beat.*)
No, I understand that that most definitely would be putting
my job a risk, of course. And I would never…
(*Beat.*)
No, of course not.
(*Beat.*)
Yes, you're right. Absolutely.
Absolutely.
That can never happen again.

SCENE EIGHT

*NED and SHARON sit facing each other on the bed. The door is closed.
They are sharing a bag of popcorn. He holds it and she dips in. She offers
him half the last handful.*

NED: No, you have it.
SHARON: No, I'm fat.
NED: You are not.
SHARON: Yes I am.
NED: I don't think you're fat.
SHARON: What d'you call this?
NED: I call it great.
SHARON: But look at it.
NED: I do.

(*He reaches out and has a squeeze.*)

SHARON: You can't do that.

NED: Why not?

SHARON: You can't squeeze my fat.

NED: It's what it's there for.

> (*He reaches out and squeezes again.*
> *She squirms and giggles.*
> *NED chases her around the bed and finally gets hold of her, pulls*
> *her into him and they hug.*)

SHARON: I had a shit day today.

NED: Why?

> (*SHARON shrugs.*)
>
> What happened?

SHARON: I lost six points.

NED: Why? What did you do?

SHARON: I didn't listen.

> Again.
>
> There's only so much I can listen to though. Before it all becomes, like, glue.
>
> They laughed at me.

NED: Who laughed at you?

SHARON: All them twats in my class.

NED: All of them?

SHARON: Well this one skinny fuck. So I jabbed him with my pencil. He was bleeding.

NED: Sharon.

SHARON: D'you hate me?

NED: Why would I hate you?

SHARON: Because I get like that.

> (*She pulls back from him.*)

NED: I done worse than you.

SHARON: Yeah? Like what?

NED: I cut someone once.

SHARON: With what?

NED: A knife.

> (*Beat.*)
>
> You hate me?
>
> (*SHARON leans in and kisses him. He kisses her back.*

GRAEME opens the door and interrupts.)

GRAEME: You said you were going to watch a video.

SHARON: In a minute.

GRAEME: Don't lie to me Sharon. You said you were going to watch a video and I believed you. Now please go and sit on the sofa like you said you would.

SHARON: Alright!

(SHARON and NED move to the sofa.)

GRAEME: Now I'm going to leave the door propped open.

(He takes the bin and is about to wedge it in the doorway.)

SHARON: What are you doing? Don't do that!

GRAEME: It's the rules.

SHARON: No I don't want you looking in.

GRAEME: I'm not looking in, I'm down the hall.

SHARON: Then what's the point of keeping it open?

GRAEME: It's the rules, Sharon.

SHARON: What's the point of rules that don't make sense?

GRAEME: Alright. We leave the door open for one, so that I can hear from down the corridor if you are in distress –

SHARON: Distress? Why would I be in distress? You're distressing me now because you won't let me close the fucking door –

GRAEME: The second reason is that it is there to remind you –

SHARON: Remind me?

GRAEME: Remind you that you are not alone. That I am here down the corridor looking out for you. And that you are not alone in here with Ned. The rules are there to protect you Sharon.

SHARON: You don't need to protect me from Ned.

GRAEME: They are to protect you from yourself.

SHARON: Fuck. Off.

(NED puts out his hand to calm her.
SHARON lies back on the sofa.)

GRAEME: Are you going to watch your video?

(SHARON shrugs.)

Ned?

NED: Yup.

(NED gets up and turns on the video player.

*GRAEME slides the bin between the door and the frame and goes
out leaving the door wedged open.*

*They sit and watch the video in silence. Suddenly SHARON gets up
and closes the door. She comes back to the sofa and sits again.)*

You shouldn't do that.

SHARON: Why not?

NED: You're just making trouble for yourself.

SHARON: I don't fucking care.

NED: Yes you do.

SHARON: Do I fuck!

NED: Sharon, you've got to understand the way they work.
You've got to learn to play their game.

SHARON: For how long? How long have I got to have a
fucking bin in my door? 'Til I leave, is that it?

NED: Sharon.

SHARON: When?

NED: I don't know.

SHARON: I want to be alone with you.

(SHARON moves to him and kisses him.

*The door swings open and GRAEME enters. He picks up a chair
and uses it to prop the door wide open, exposing them to the
entire hallway.)*

You can't do that!

(GRAEME turns to go.)

Use the bin. I won't move the bin!

(GRAEME spins round.)

GRAEME: You did already. Now I don't trust you, do I? You
can earn my trust again by not moving this chair. Then I'll
let you put the bin back in its place.

SHARON: No!

GRAEME: Yes. I need to trust you, or I can't leave you alone.

SHARON: Leave me alone!

GRAEME: If you don't want to watch a video you could play a
board game. Would you like that? Or some cards?

SHARON: I don't want to play cards, do I?

GRAEME: I'll get you some cards.

(GRAEME goes out leaving the door propped wide open.

SHARON paces the room.)

NED: It's alright Sharon.

SHARON: No.

I don't want to play *cards* with you.

(*GRAEME comes back with the cards and hands them to her.*
She turns her back on him.
NED takes the cards.
GRAEME goes out, leaving the door propped wide open.
SHARON is shaking with fury and frustration.)

NED: Come on.

(*He sits on the floor.*)

You know Snap?

SHARON: Fuck this.

(*NED deals the cards into two neat piles.*
SHARON paces.)

(*Shouts into the corridor.*) Fuck!

(*SHARON kicks the bottom of the chair, mainly for show.*
NED shuffles his half of the pack.
SHARON loiters at the back of the room.
*NED shuffles her half of the pack and places them neatly down
opposite each other and waits.*
And waits.
*Eventually SHARON comes to sit in front of him. She picks up
her pack and they play.*
NED puts one down.)

NED: Now you put one down.

SHARON: I know!

NED: Well do it then.

(*SHARON slams a card down.*
NED slams another. And so on until…)

SHARON: SNAP!

(*She grabs the pile and draws it into her.*)

NED: Come on then.

(*SHARON slams down another. They whip through the cards.*
*They go a couple of rounds of aggressive play until they 'SNAP' at
the same time and SHARON grabs onto his hand. After a moment
NED unlocks his hand and takes up his cards.*)

Come on.

(*SHARON takes up her cards. They play another couple of rounds.*
NED wins them both.)

SHARON: You're too fast!

NED: You've got to concentrate.

> (*Every time NED 'SNAPS', SHARON copies and slams her hand down on top of his, grabbing his fingers and holding onto them. He repeatedly untangles his hand and carries on play. This happens until SHARON is so red-faced with frustration that she chucks her pack across the room and her cards fly everywhere.*
> *They sit staring at each other.*
> *Suddenly she lashes out at him, but he blocks her and holds her firmly. She folds into his arms. He rocks her.*
> *GRAEME comes to the doorway and watches them.*)

GRAEME: Ned.

> (*NED won't let her go.*)
> Ned.
> (*NED slowly lifts her off him and pushes her away.*)
> Thank you.

SCENE NINE

NED is mopping the hallway. GRAEME approaches.

GRAEME: Hi Ned.

NED: Hello.

GRAEME: Do you have time for a quick word?

NED: Now?

GRAEME: Yes, now.

NED: Sure. What it is?

GRAEME: It's Sharon, Ned.

NED: She alright?

GRAEME: Yes she's fine. I want to talk about you and Sharon. I know that you've got to like spending time together.

NED: Yeah.

GRAEME: Well, you know how it is then, don't you? You remember from when you were here.

> (*Beat.*)
> Sharon's not like you.

NED: Yes she is.

GRAEME: No. She's not. She's only sixteen. She's three years
    behind you. She's three years behind you. She doesn't listen. She doesn't co-operate. She
    hasn't learnt –

NED: She's angry.

GRAEME: I know.

NED: No you don't.

GRAEME: I'm sorry?

NED: You don't know.

    (*Beat.*)

GRAEME: I've trained, Ned. I'm trained to help people like
    Sharon, alright? She has a lot to learn. And she can't have
    any influences that are unreliable.

NED: But I'm not unreliable.

GRAEME: That's right, you're very good at your job. You work
    hard. You've come a long way. You've come a long way,
    Ned, from where you were. And I know you don't want
    to go back there. I know you value your job and that you
    wouldn't do anything to put that in jeopardy.

NED: Why would my job be in jeopardy?

GRAEME: I didn't say it was. I said I know you wouldn't do
    anything to put it in jeopardy because you're reliable.

    (*Beat.*)

NED: I love her. She's the best thing I ever... I want to take
    care of her.

GRAEME: We are all trying to take care of her, Ned. But what
    Sharon needs is structure. And friends. Friends to help her
    grow. Sharon needs to grow up. You remember. You were
    there. You remember the person you were. You remember
    the things that you did.

    (*Beat.*)

    Can you be a friend to Sharon?

    (*Beat.*)

    Please think about it.

    (*GRAEME walks away.*

    NED stands breathing hard. All of a sudden he violently drives
    his fist into the wall. He retracts his hand and stares at his fist
    before bringing it up to his face.)

SCENE TEN

SHARON sits in her room waiting for NED. He knocks on the door.
She runs to it and opens it, she launches in for her hug and kiss but he
quickly disengages.

SHARON: What's wrong?

NED: Nothing.

SHARON: Why won't you kiss me? I've been dying for a kiss
   all day.

   (*NED moves the chair to prop open the door.*)

   What are you doing?

NED: Putting the chair here.

SHARON: Why?

NED: Because, you know.

SHARON: Yeah but Graeme's not here yet. Give us a couple of
   minutes won't it.

   (*She begins to move the chair.*)

NED: Don't Sharon.

SHARON: Why not?

   (*Beat.*)

   What's the matter?

NED: I brought a video.

SHARON: So did I.

NED: Oh right, what?

   (*SHARON produces an unmarked VHS.*)

   What is it?

SHARON: Porn.

NED: What?

SHARON: I got it from this guy in my class.

   D'you want to watch it with me?

   (*Beat.*)

NED: No.

   (*GRAEME can be heard coming down the hall. He enters.*)

GRAEME: You going to watch a video then?

NED: Yes.

GRAEME: Good. What are you going to watch?

   (*SHARON holds the video behind her back.*)

   What is that video Sharon?

89

SHARON: Nothing.

GRAEME: Give it to me.

SHARON: No.

GRAEME: What is this Ned?

NED: It's nothing. It's nothing to do with me. I didn't know she was going to… I don't want to watch that video with her.

SHARON: Ned?

GRAEME: Ned can you come with me please?

SHARON: No! No I'm sorry. Ned. I'm sorry. Wait! Have it. I won't watch it. We can watch your video. Ned brought a video.

GRAEME: What video did you bring Ned?

NED: 'Pirates of the Caribbean.'

SHARON: I love that. Can we watch that? Please. Ned.
    (*Beat.*)

GRAEME: You can watch Ned's video but I can't leave you alone. I'm sorry Sharon, I just can't. I'm going have to supervise you.

SHARON: No!

GRAEME: You give me no choice.
    (*SHARON suddenly throws her video at the wall. They all stand in silence.*)
    You do that again and Ned won't be allowed to see you.

SHARON: Fuck you!

GRAEME: Don't you see that you could have hurt someone!

SHARON: I don't care!

GRAEME: Sharon. Please. I am trying to give you every opportunity to exercise self-control.
    Now, you can watch Ned's video but I will supervise. There is no argument.
    (*SHARON shakes.*
    NED takes a seat on the sofa.)
    Sharon.
    (*SHARON takes a seat on the sofa. GRAEME follows.*)

SHARON: No!

GRAEME: Don't shout.

SHARON: You're not allowed on the sofa. You have to sit out there.

GRAEME: Fine.

(*GRAEME takes the bin and goes out into the corridor, leaving the chair propping open the door. He turns the bin upside down and sits on it, looking in.*

NED goes to the video player.)

SHARON: Ned?

(*NED inserts the video.*)

Ned?

(*NED presses play. The video plays.*

He comes to the sofa and sits a distance from her.

SHARON watches NED. NED watches the video.

Suddenly SHARON takes NED's hand, he withdraws it.

She takes his hand again, he untangles it.)

GRAEME: Sharon. Watch the video.

(*SHARON slams the side of the sofa and almost immediately reaches out and grabs his hand. They struggle.*)

Sharon. I can see you. Let go of him.

Sharon.

NED: Sharon, let go of me.

GRAEME: Let go of him Sharon.

(*SHARON pulls away and wrenches herself off the sofa.*)

SHARON: (*To GRAEME.*) Go away!

(*GRAEME stands.*

SHARON comes to move the chair.)

GRAEME: Sharon if you move that chair…

(*SHARON takes hold of the chair.*)

Don't move that chair!

(*SHARON pushes the chair into the centre of the room.*

GRAEME jumps off the bin and catches the door, holding it open.)

Bring it back.

SHARON: This fucking chair!

NED: Sharon.

SHARON: I hate this chair!

GRAEME: It's alright Sharon.

SHARON: No. It's not alright!

GRAEME: Please calm down.

SHARON: I hate this chair! I hate this place!

NED: Sharon. Sharon? It's alright Sharon.

SHARON: This fucking… I can't…

GRAEME: Sharon. Please calm down.

You're going to hurt someone.

SHARON: Me. I can't. I. I.

I hate. I hate this fucking chair!

(*SHARON takes hold of the chair as if she might throw it against the wall but instead straddles the chair as though it were a man and begins to simulate having sex with it.*)

GRAEME: Sharon. Sharon, stop it.

(*But SHARON continues, becoming lost in the rhythm of it. NED stares at her, torn.*

Soon he stands and comes towards the chair.)

Ned.

(*He gets onto the floor, lies down on his back and slides himself under the chair so that he is looking up at her.*)

Ned. Sharon. Stop –

(*GRAEME stays in the doorway as they both rock violently to and fro with the chair between them until they are exhausted. And when they are done, SHARON lowers her arm to NED over the back of the chair, and he reaches up and takes her hand.*

The End.)

Sarah Cuddon
WEIGHTLESS

Characters

BETH

DOCTOR

JACK

Weightless was first performed on 6 April 2007 as part of the HighTide Festival at The Cut in Halesworth, Suffolk, with the following company:

BETH, Jennifer Kidd
DOCTOR, Celia Adams
JACK, Charlie Roe

Director Rachel Grunwald
Designers Josephine Callaghan
          Tanya Cunningham
Lighting Designer Lawrence Stromski
Sound Designer Steve Mayo

Interior. BETH is standing on a chair painting a wall. 'Let's go crazy' by Prince plays on the radio. BETH stops every now and then to dance. Her attention is caught by a radio advert which fades up over the music.

RADIO: The man in tiny pants, the artist known as Prince and 'Let's Go Crazy'. Now fasten your seat-belts all you aspiring astronauts out there because the Soviet Space administration is offering one of you an opportunity to motor down the Milky Way. No experience necessary. So if you want to blast off on the tripski of a lifetime call
(*BETH starts to search for a pen and paper. She can't find one so she paints the number on the wall.*)
0800 456 7298, that's 0800 456 7298… Take it away Nina…
('*I wish I knew how it would feel to be free' by Nina Simone comes up on the radio. BETH continues to paint the walls painting carefully around the number. The light whitens. Music fades. BETH appears to go into a trance. She starts to walk on the spot as if space walking. Lights fade. Lights up. It is the day of the launch. Star City, Russia. BETH is joined by the DOCTOR who is carrying out routine medical checks.*)
BETH: Do you ever get that feeling…
DOCTOR: And look to the right…
BETH: You want to run into a wall…
DOCTOR: And the left….
BETH: Or a pillar…
DOCTOR: Up to the ceiling…
BETH: Just run. Full speed.
DOCTOR: Your arm please.
    (*She takes BETH's blood pressure.*)
BETH: Smack.
DOCTOR: Good.
BETH: Yes? You know that feeling?
DOCTOR: No.

BETH: You must. Say you're driving on an open road, the temptation to rev the car up and fire off the end of something.

DOCTOR: I don't drive a car.

BETH: Okay. What about standing on a bridge? Or at the top of a flight of stairs and you see yourself trip and fall bang, bang, bang, to the bottom?

DOCTOR: Maybe. Yes. The stairs. I know that feeling when you're on the stairs. Or an escalator.

BETH: Yes, an escalator. Or a cliff top. When you're just inches from the edge and there's no railing just the…

DOCTOR: Please Beth. Enough. You can say these things to a psychiatrist but I'm a doctor. I don't want to be putting you in a straight-jacket today okay? Today you go high and you don't fall.

BETH: Right. I float. I let go and I float but beneath me is a whole load of nothing for hundreds and hundreds of miles. How do you ever come back to stairs and cars once you've been up there?

DOCTOR: Sometimes it's hard to come back. Sometimes you find God. Many cosmonauts think they've found God up there. It helps them.

BETH: If I find God I'm not coming back.

DOCTOR: (*Looking in her leather case.*) Okay. Now I have a nose-clip for you here.

BETH: I really find it difficult to wear those.

DOCTOR: When you are up there you will want this. Everything is floating in weightless conditions. Bits of food, bits of how do you say? Whiskers? Bits of skin… So much dust.

BETH: (*Speaking with the nose-clip on.*) It's suffocating.

DOCTOR: You choose. Either you wear it or you sneeze a lot. And when I say a lot I mean maybe thirty times an hour. Seriously. (*Pause.*) Okay so in a little while you have the final body sterilization. Then you will have the last breakfast before you take off.

BETH: Makes it sound like death row. The last breakfast.

DOCTOR: Meat stew, bread, pickled vegetables, porridge, cream...vodka. Russian breakfast *is* like death.

BETH: (*Moving to look out of the window.*) I've got a secret store of muesli.

DOCTOR: Ahh the English bird food. Much better.

BETH: Window ledges. That's another one. I used to climb onto them when I was a child and just sit there dangling my legs and I'd see myself nosedive onto the ground. Out. Cold. Then I'd pick myself up and do it again but this time I'd fall like a leaf or a feather. You know the way they duck backwards and forwards.

(*BETH holds her hand out to see if it's shaking. The DOCTOR walks over to her, takes both BETH's hands in her own and moves her away from the window.*)

Shall we turn the radio on? I want to hear what they're saying.

(*The DOCTOR turns on the radio and tries tuning in to various stations.*)

DOCTOR: Nothing yet. (*She moves to turn it off.*)

BETH: No, leave it on. I like it. Reminds me of long car journeys at night. Tucked up on the back seat with the radio on...

(*Lights down on BETH and the DOCTOR. Time shifts back one year. BETH is a couple of months into training for the mission. Lights up on JACK who is sitting at a table writing. There is a pile of books next to him. A teapot, a cup and a radio are also on the table. Music plays faintly on the radio. JACK turns the radio off and lifts the tea-cosy. As he speaks he enjoys the ritual of a cup of tea. Pouring a cup. Adding milk, then sugar. Stirring. Tasting. Adding some more milk. Periodically we can see he is in some pain.*)

JACK: Always feels as if you should be pouring for two. When you make a pot. (*Pause.*) 'Have you met my daughter? She's training to become an astronaut. An astronaut. Yes. My daughter.' Watched Aldrin and Armstrong landing on the moon and never thought... Couldn't have imagined this. I'd just bought our first TV. Second-hand. Absolute crap. If you moved, the picture just conked out. Mum had just died so you must have been six and we just sat there watching the 'giant leap' with our mouths open. Next day you came home from school with a shuttle made out of milk bottle tops. You started making rockets out of your bloody mashed potato, God, and then you wouldn't eat it…because it was now a 'rocket'. You couldn't understand why the stars didn't come into your bedroom at night if you left your window open. So I told you you should go and sleep out in the garden if you really wanted stars.

(*He takes a bottle of pills from his pocket, removes a couple and lines them up on the table before downing them one by one with his tea.*)

They say it sounds like the sky's being ripped apart when a shuttle launches. You can feel it. Like a fist pounding right here (*He pounds his fist on his chest, coughs and takes a sip of tea.*) Bit tepid. Not good when it's tepid. Should be piping hot.

(*Lights fade. BETH joins JACK at the table. She is playing a game of Patience. She is fast and absorbed. JACK opens a bottle of wine, pours two glasses and offers one to BETH, who refuses it. JACK returns to the end of the table and picks up his book. We can still see the patch of wall where BETH painted the telephone number.*)

BETH: Five on six, seven on eight, four on three…

(*She finishes her game and looks up at JACK. She takes the cards, shuffles them, fans the deck and holds them out to him.*)

Pick a card.

(*No response.*)

Dad?

JACK: Umm. What?

BETH: Pick a card. Go on. Any card.

(*He takes a card.*)

Okay. Now have a look. Remember that card. Got it? Now put it back. Anywhere. Okay.

(*She shuffles the pack, splits it in two. Takes the top card from one of the two piles, holds it up and smiles.*)

JACK: Very smooth.

BETH: 'Men love a woman who can conjure a trick Beth.'

JACK: Did I really feed you that line?

BETH: Yes. I was seven.

JACK: Worked on that dentist boyfriend of yours.

BETH: Until I told him how to do it. Then he buggered off.

JACK: He was always looking at my teeth.

BETH: You're just paranoid about your teeth.

JACK: I've got good teeth. (*Pause.*) You taking a pack of cards up in the shuttle?

BETH: I'm not through yet.

JACK: Oh come on Beth. You're flying through these tests.

BETH: And the other candidates hate it. All ex-army blokes. Pumped up to the eyeballs with ego. They swagger round like they're masters of the universe. I can read what they're thinking like it's tattooed on their foreheads: 'A woman's place is on Mother Earth.'

JACK: They're probably all falling in love with you.

BETH: No Dad. That's not it. Why do you always think that? No it's just they get this awful patronising look on their faces like: 'This is going to be difficult for you. Especially the enemas. But we're used to that sort of thing.'

JACK: Well they're ex-army. Of course they're used to it. Always sticking probes up you. We used to have something called Procto-prep before a flight. Everyone competing to see who could get the cleanest colon.

BETH: Dad please.

JACK: Don't be prudish. Now tell me about this centrifuge. I want to know how it works.

BETH: It simulates G-force.

JACK: Yes I know that.

BETH: You've got this small cage with a seat in it and it spins around the room. It's like something out of James Bond. So you're strapped in there and there's an instructor telling you to close your eyes and tip your head up and down until you feel your stomach contract.
(*JACK is half listening and leafing through a book looking for something.*)
A lot of people black out but... Dad?

JACK: Yes. I'm listening.

BETH: …but you can control it by tensing your abdomen muscles so you keep blood in the brain. If you're about to black out your vision starts to blur and you get this grey curtain coming in from the sides. But if you tense up really tight you can make it go away. So you hold your breath. Tense. Relax. It's incredibly powerful. And I can do it. I'm good at it.

JACK: (*Reading from a book.*) Here it is, yes. 'The centrifuge places an immense amount of pressure on the torso and brain resulting in the genuine sensation of a rocket launch and a psychotic grin appearing on the face of the candidate.'

BETH: I'm trying to tell you about it.

JACK: I'm listening.

BETH: What *is* that book?

JACK: Yuri Gagarin's biography.

BETH: Why are you reading that?

JACK: I'm curious. Soviet cosmonaut. First human to orbit the earth.

(*BETH is evidently annoyed.*)

Almost impossible to upset him apparently.

BETH: Who?

JACK: Yuri Gagarin.

BETH: Yuri Gagarin. Right.

JACK: Yes.

(*JACK is looking for something in a book again. BETH is irritated.*)

'The whole of mankind stood to gain from Gagarin's breakthrough in space because it brought the planet closer together.'

(*Silence. BETH takes the pack of cards and starts to shuffle them fast. JACK takes a bottle of pills from his pocket, discreetly removes a couple and downs them one by one. BETH is playing Patience again but watches him from the corner of her eyes.*)

BETH: You still getting chest pains?

JACK: Here and there.

BETH: Maybe you should lay off the red wine for a bit.

JACK: You sound like a school teacher.

BETH: You're starting to look like a wino. (*Pause.*) You should get your hair cut.

JACK: You used to like it when it got long.

BETH: It just looks limp.

JACK: Even if I do this? (*He ruffles his hair.*)

BETH: You look like a scarecrow.

JACK: You're hard to please aren't you.

BETH: What are you writing at the moment?

JACK: Oh nothing much. Just bits and pieces.

> (*Silence. BETH continues to play cards. JACK watches her.*)
> (*Trying to make conversation.*) I saw that colleague of yours from Mars today. Kate was it?

BETH: I don't want to think about Mars.

JACK: They were all given a bonus last week. She said the story about that rock star…what's his name…Mick Jagger…eating a Mars Bar from between some girl's legs… Hit the headlines again and sales went up. Ridiculous.

BETH: Mars is over. I'm not at Mars anymore. I don't want to think about Mars. I've left that little bar of turd behind me. But everyone's always reminding me about it. I don't find it very funny anymore. The joke. You know, Beth Eades used to work for Mars incorporated and now she might be off into the Milky Way. The galaxy could be hers ha ha ha.
> (*Lights fade down on JACK during BETH's monologue.*)
When I heard that ad on the radio I could hardly bear to even look at a Mars bar. My fingers always smelt of them. And I could hear you saying, 'Write that number down Beth. Just write it down. You can do that. Time to move on. Throw caution to the wind.' (*Pause.*) But you know it used to be you who leapt at things. *You* were the soldier who jumped from boats and planes. *You* were the one who rode a motorbike like it was a rocket. My dad's Steve McQueen. Made me so proud. I could never keep up with you though. First time I got on a horse you came up behind and gave it a huge smack on the arse so it bolted and I just had to hang on for my life. And the way you used to storm ahead when we went climbing. I'd be hanging on the edge of some cliff face and you could never hear me yelling, 'Stop. Will you just wait a minute. I can't keep up with

you.' I cannot imagine you climbing mountains these days. You're so distracted. I'm sure you've got shorter. You spend too much time at that table. (*Pause.*) 'When an organism stops exploring its environment, it means it's beginning to die.' You told me that. You told me that.

(*Lights up on JACK.*)

JACK: Pissing blood. I've been pissing blood and that's not good. No. That just won't do. Horrified by my curiosity. The urge to record every damn step of this illness. Write it out of me. Long suspected it might be incurable but… I can't decide whether I should be angry or dismissive. Do I say: 'Come here you little fucker, I'm going to kick you from one end of the room to the other'? Or: 'Oh God, you're so tedious, just piss off while I get on with my life'? Then that desire for some sort of expanse. Some wilderness. To break out again. To stand at the top of a mountain or in the eye of a storm. I've always thought it would be rather magnificent to be struck dead by lightning. A single blow from the sky. So much more noble than watching yourself wither. Noble and bizarre. (*Pause.*) We should have had another child. We should have given you a brother or a sister. (*Pause.*) Watching you talk about the mission there is such passion in you. You've got the face of a heroine. Quite beautiful. It's the face I used to have.

(*Lights up on BETH.*)

BETH: The stairs. That space between bed and sleep and all the life of the kitchen. There's a lot that feels possible when you're sitting on the stairs. Not quite here. Not quite there. I used to sit with my head against the banister and listen to you talking to yourself. I could time it. By about nine o'clock you'd had a few glasses of wine and you'd be mumbling, bollocks, stuff, just chatting away. I'd take my seat in the gods and try and tune in. And most of the time it was indecipherable. Just grunts and mutters. But sometimes I could pull out a sentence and it became so compulsive just trying to hear something, anything. Something about Mum or about me. I remember you saying, 'At the end of the day what do you remember, what do you really remember?' and then you got up and slammed your fist on the table and said, 'I'd like to fuck you in your stilettos, just you and a pair of stilettos.' That was it. It really shocked me, in an exciting way. I think I was only about nine. But I wanted you to carry on. I wanted to hear more of that part of you. The bit I didn't know. So many bits of you I don't know.

(*Lights up on JACK.*)

JACK: She might find God. Why do they all come back born-again Christians? The ones who get as far as the moon, they all come back Christians or alcoholics. But that's right isn't it? It should be hard. Bloody hard. When you've hit zero gravity. The jolt. Must feel as if your soul's left your body. Like the split second as you leave the door of the plane and your stomach turns inside out. Whoosh. We'd be sitting there in the open door almost catatonic and they'd have to boot us out. Those brutes yelling, 'Go. Go. You. Go. Now.' You were programmed to react to the word 'go' so you did it. You just leapt. Sucked into the slip-stream. Great feeling, unless you were being shot at. And then that huge tug on your shoulders and the parachute exploding above you as though some mighty hand was dragging you upwards.

(*Lights fade. BETH is standing at the end of the table where JACK usually sits. She is looking through some of the books he has piled there. She picks up his notebook and starts to read it. She is evidently shocked and distressed by its contents. She spends some time leafing through the book. Lights down. Just a radio is illuminated. A radio report fades up.*)

RADIO: Twenty-eight year-old Beth Eades has beaten thousands of applicants and passed months of rigorous tests to join the next Soviet Space Mission. Until ten months ago Beth was working as a food technologist for Mars confectioners. Now the galaxy is her Milky Way and she's left Mars light years behind her. It seems outer space is getting closer to home and you don't need superhuman powers to get there…

(*Lights up on BETH and JACK.*)

BETH: I can't go on the mission.

JACK: What?

BETH: I can't go on the mission.

JACK: Let's just sit down a moment here Beth…

BETH: I looked in one of your books. I'm sorry. I know I shouldn't have. But I just picked it up and I read some of it. I thought it was a book of ideas…for stories or something. But it was almost illegible. Not even words in some bits, just scrawls. I thought maybe it was that doodling you do but there were pages and pages of it. Why are you writing like that? What's the matter?

JACK: Beth you didn't have any right to do that. That is private.

BETH: But I did look and I saw it… What is it? Explain it to me. The mad writing. I could hardly read it except for odd words…like nausea. You kept writing nausea. Nausea over and over again. Has it got worse? Your heart. What is it? Please tell me Dad.

JACK: You know what it is Beth. I've got a little bit of heart trouble and the medication makes me feel nauseous. You know that.

BETH: Dad, please. Tell me the truth. You've got thinner and you just don't do very much. Just sit behind all those books.

JACK: You're not supposed to do very much if you've got a dicky heart. That's why I'm not doing very much Beth. I have to take things slowly these days. I can't do much.

BETH: (*Distressed and shaking her head.*) No.

JACK: They're good, the doctors. I'm in good hands and I'm…you know…I'm on the up.

BETH: The writing though…

JACK: The writing is my writing and it is private. I'm sorry if it disturbed you. It's… Look. Beth. The mission, your training, you're about to enter an extraordinary world. You cannot possibly give that up. You'd be making a huge mistake if you did that. And it really isn't necessary.

BETH: I've been so wrapped up in it all I haven't been paying attention to what's happening though. You look sad.

JACK: Of course you've been wrapped up in it. That's right. That's what I brought you up to do. To be an adventurer. And you are. Passionately so. You'll take your seat in that shuttle because that's what you were born to do Beth. You were. I can't climb mountains…at the moment. But I can watch you go. And you know that's almost better. You! Bolting into space. That's a glorious idea. Isn't it? Isn't it? (*BETH is silent.*)
You must go. I want that. I'll be fine. Please don't give this up.
(*BETH and JACK embrace. Lights down. Lights up. Interior, Star City. BETH is being given the final body sterilization by the DOCTOR.*)

DOCTOR: Men lie and they don't know they are lying. They believe it's the truth. And they lie especially about their health. Because they're terrified of someone else telling them they are ill and they must take some medicine. So we have to take responsibility. We have to watch out for them as well as for ourselves. Otherwise they would all be dying off and that would be such a shame.

BETH: I don't want the responsibility.

DOCTOR: Well no, maybe you don't want it. But you take it, because you're a woman and we do that.

BETH: I used to walk through walls.

DOCTOR: What do you mean?

BETH: If I felt I needed to escape responsibility, I used to imagine I could walk through the wall.

DOCTOR: A hallucination?

BETH: I suppose so. But sometimes it would feel absolutely real. I made a picture fall from my shelf once just by staring at it.

DOCTOR: Your face looks strange.

BETH: Do you want to have children?

DOCTOR: Yes. I want children.

BETH: How many?

DOCTOR: Two maybe.

BETH: Why two?

DOCTOR: One is lonely.

BETH: Yes. One can be lonely.

DOCTOR: You feel lonely?

BETH: Not today, no. Sometimes. I feel lonely when I think of my father. I feel lonely *for* him when I think what I'm about to do. He should be here today.

DOCTOR: Beth, please. Let me remind you of something important. A few years ago there was another mission. Soyuz 11. Three cosmonauts. Twenty-four days in space. The longest time anyone has remained weightless. It was a great achievement. Then the spacecraft returned to earth. We have a record of the men talking as they came back. An old woman and a cow were the first to see the spacecraft land. Then people arrived to help the cosmonauts out. They opened the…you know the hatch and the three men were still strapped in their seats. Cold. They died maybe just minutes after landing. All of them were married and they had children. (*Pause.*) I want to say to you. You are a clever woman. You have exceptional strength. You are leaving very soon. It is a dangerous thing you are about to do. You never get into a shuttle without saying goodbye just before you go.

(*The DOCTOR takes a bottle of vodka and two shot glasses from her leather case and pours it. They drink. Lights fade slightly. BETH stands up and kisses the DOCTOR. Lights remain on BETH. Lights up on JACK.*)

BETH: It's so quiet here and I'm just waiting. How are you Dad?

JACK: I'm bearing up.

BETH: And the pains?

JACK: They're the same. Not too bad. (*Pause.*) I'm trying to get a picture of you out there.

BETH: Well, it's very white Star City and very sterile and I'm… It's a bit hard to describe it. I keep looking at the sky as if it might tell me something. But it's just the sky.

JACK: Very odd not to be there with you.

BETH: You'll probably get a better picture on TV anyway.

JACK: Shame they can't connect me up to your shuttle with some sort of satellite thing.

BETH: I'm scared Dad.

JACK: No you're not. You're perfectly calm. (*Pause.*) Look out for New Zealand. It's supposed to look fabulous from up there.

BETH: New Zealand. Yes.

JACK: Smells of spring here today. Freshly cut grass in the air. I had a thought. Pick a handful of grass to take with you will you. There won't be much to smell up there. I'm sure Russian grass doesn't smell as good as English grass but...

BETH: I'll take some grass. Yes. And you hold back on the red wine.

JACK: Oh yes. I'll have kicked that habit when you get back.

BETH: Look up at the sky sometimes.

JACK: I'll be there Beth. At the end of the garden.

(*Lights down. Lights up on BETH.*)

BETH: *You must go Beth. I want that.* Right up until the last minute I could feel my conviction wavering. Right up until the moment I saw the shuttle. There it was. Solid and grey. So purposeful and serene. I felt this rush of respect for it. White condensation poured off it and rolled down the sides. It was like a living creature. (*Pause.*) I must have scratched my hands really hard with my nails as we took off because they were bleeding when I next looked at them. We were about two hundred and fifty miles up and I took my first look out of the window over the Pacific Ocean. I could see the curve of the earth. The water was this bright blue with brilliant white clouds coasting over the top and the sunlight was streaming. It was like looking at a moving globe. It took about the length of time it takes to watch a film to circle the earth once. On the first night up there we spotted these patches glowing bright orange. The fires in the oil-fields in Kuwait. They were still burning. You can't see man-made features from that distance unless they're in straight lines. Cities are a blur. Bare earth is brown or red. I only saw two places that looked green; Ireland and the South Island of New Zealand. You were right, New Zealand is luminous. The night sky looked like someone had spattered it with white paint. And there were these electric storms. One lightning flash would

explode and set off another flash, which set off another somewhere else, like this chain reaction in silver. It would spread for hundreds of miles, but people on earth would have no idea of the scale of it because they'd only see a tiny part. (*Pause.*) I spent hours just looking down on the earth and thinking, 'That's my planet but it's not my world anymore.' You can't see individuals, or their relationships, or their illnesses. You just see the land where they exist. My brain felt slow and a bit sticky. I had these recurring visions. I gave birth to a baby. A tiny foetus made of bark and once it was born it was just sucked away into the black. And then my womb flew out as well. It just spun out of my body. A flying womb whirling into space. It was almost comical. (*Pause.*) You're connected to the shuttle by an umbilical hose which has radio wires in it so you can communicate with the spacecraft. When I made my first exit all my internal organs seemed to turn over and I swear my heart got bigger. I was somersaulting and the earth was moving under me like running water. It was so much better out of the shuttle because there were no window frames. You could see a full one hundred and eighty degrees. Every thing looks perfect far away. And the weightlessness, the weightlessness was the most natural, relaxing feeling I'd ever known. It was like swimming in liquid silk. The umbilical hose floating away from me and the radio ticking blip, blip, blip. My shape scrawled in the air. Like that white trail you get just after a sparkler's gone out. I didn't want to return to the shuttle. I could just loosen the hose and glide away.
(*Lights down.*
The End.)